DURCH STARTEN

ENGLISCH GRAMMATIK

9 bis 12

COACHINGBUCH

VerfasserInnen: Sonja Häusler, Katrin Pürer, Franz Zach
Mitarbeit: Catherine Spring, Edward Woolner

Diesem Buch ist ein Lösungsheft zu den Übungen beigelegt.

Entspricht der Rechtschreibreform 2006

Bibliografische Information der Deutschen Bibliothek:
Die Deutsche Bibliothek verzeichnet diese Publikation in der Deutschen Nationalbibliografie; detaillierte bibliografische Daten sind im Internet über http://dnb.ddb.de abrufbar.

VERITAS-VERLAG, Linz
www.veritas.at

Lektorat: Klaus Kopinitsch
Grafische Gestaltung: Gottfried Moritz, Julia Dresch
Illustrationen: Stefan Stratil
Satz: Harald Leiter
Herstellung: Julia Dresch

4. Auflage 2018 ISBN 978-3-7101-0233-2

VERITAS
Gemeinsam besser lernen

Inhaltsverzeichnis

HELLO! WELCOME TO ENGLISH GRAMMAR!

Zu allererst ...

Herzlich willkommen in der Oberstufe! Vier Jahre liegen vor dir, an deren Ende der Lohn für viel Mühe und Fleiß steht: die Matura. Diese ist mittlerweile österreichweit zentral und besteht aus den Teilen **Leseveständnis**, **Hörverständnis**, **Sprache im Kontext** und zwei **Schreibteilen**. Falls du dich nun fragst, warum wir dir das alles erzählen und was überhaupt so besonders an der vorliegenden Oberstufengrammatik ist, lies einfach weiter!

Warum?

Grammatikbücher gibt es ja mittlerweile fast wie Sand am Meer. Die meisten sind allerdings für die Unterstufe vorgesehen und gespickt mit Einsetzübungen, um die erlernten Grammatikaspekte zu üben und zu automatisieren. Das ist gut und daran gibt es überhaupt nichts auszusetzten! Das Schwierige ist allerdings die Tatsache, dass dich diese Art der Übungen nicht optimal auf die Zentralmatura – genauer gesagt auf den Bereich **Language in Use** (Sprache/Sprachverwendung im Kontext) vorbereitet. Hier geht es nämlich darum, erlernte Grammatikkenntnisse gekonnt, sicher und flexibel im Kontext verschiedener Texte richtig anzuwenden.

Wie?

Idealerweise begleitet dich die vorliegende Oberstufengrammatik durch die ganzen vier Jahre bis hin zur Matura. Die Inhalte (A, B, C ...) in weinroter Farbe auf (meist) linken Buchseiten sind in **drei Abschnitte** (**Schwierigkeitsgrade**) gegliedert, welche durch ! optisch gekennzeichnet und gut erkennbar sind. Die Übungen (1, 2, 3 ...) in gelber Farbe sind diesen drei unterschiedlichen Schwierigkeitsniveaus zugeordnet. Inhalte und Übungen umfassen daher folgende Kategorien:

A 1 ***elementary***

... besonders geeignet für SchülerInnen der 9. Schulstufe (5. Klasse AHS), um die Unterstufengrammatik (also die Grundgrammatik) zu wiederholen und zu vertiefen.

A 1 ! ***intermediate***

... besonders geeignet für SchülerInnen der 10./11. Schulstufe (6./7. Klasse AHS), um die Grammatik in einfachen Language in Use-Übungen anzuwenden und sich mit den Maturaformaten schrittweise vertraut zu machen.

A 1 !! ***advanced***

... besonders geeignet für SchülerInnen der 11./12. Schulstufe (7./8. Klasse AHS), um optimal und effizient auf die bevorstehende Zentralmatura (insbesondere Language in Use) hinzuarbeiten.

Zum Schluss ...

... bleibt nur noch, dir viel Erfolg und Motivation auf deinem Weg zur Zentralmatura zu wünschen!

All the best,
Sonja Häusler, Katrin Pürer & Franz Zach ☺

ADJECTIVE – EIGENSCHAFTSWORT

Das Adjektiv (Eigenschaftswort) sagt uns, wie etwas ist oder zu sein scheint. Es beschreibt somit die Eigenschaft von Menschen, Dingen und Tieren und nicht deren Handlungen.

A Grundsätzliches zum Adjektiv

Das Adjektiv steht:

nach bestimmten Verben, welche Eigenschaften oder Zustände beschreiben:	**vor dem Nomen**, dessen Eigenschaft es beschreibt:
*This **is** so **typical** of you!*	*Horst is a **typical German**.*
*The idea **sounds interesting**.*	*That's an **interesting situation**.*
*You **look horrible** today, Ben!*	*Ben is in a **horrible mood** today.*
*The first question **appeared easy**.*	*That's an **easy question**!*
Zu diesen Verben zählen: • alle Formen von ***to be*** • ***appear, feel, look, smell, seem, sound, taste*** • ***become, get, go, grow, turn,*** wenn sie „werden" bedeuten	Niemals vor einem Nomen stehen **ill** (krank) und **well** (gesund): *an **ill** person → a **sick** person* *a **well** person → a **healthy** person*
Für mehr Information dazu siehe Kapitel ADVERBS, Abschitt D, Seite 22.	aber: *You **look ill**, Maria. **Get well** soon.*

B *word order* bei mehreren Adjektiven

1. Wenn zur näheren Beschreibung eines Nomens mehr als ein Adjektiv verwendet wird, dann gilt diese Reihenfolge:

„Meinung vor Tatsache" oder	**„subjektiv vor objektiv"**
*a **boring old** story*	*a **beautiful gothic** church*
*a **nice young** teacher*	*an **excellent new** movie*

2. Werden mehrere „objektive" Eigenschaften genannt, dann gilt diese Reihenfolge:

	Größe	Alter	Farbe	Herkunft	Material	
some	***big***	***old***		***American***		*cars*
a	***small***		***red***		***rubber***	*ball*
my		***new***	***brown***	***Italian***	***leather***	*handbag*

1 Complete the sentences with the adjectives in brackets.

EXAMPLE This is a really **easy** *(einfach)* exercise, don't you think so?

1. Last weekend something .... *(wunderbar)* happened:
   I got a .... *(klein)* brown puppy for my birthday!
2. I love English even though it's a bit .... *(schwierig)*.
3. Pam thinks it's .... *(verrückt)* to watch the same movie twice.
4. I have to admit that your ideas sound .... *(interessant)*.
5. We definitely need a .... *(verlässlich)* person for this job!
6. Have you ever heard of aliens or other .... *(seltsam)* creatures?
7. Ms Porter, our new English teacher, is really .... *(streng)*.
8. Mum, I'm so .... *(müde)* I can hardly keep going.
9. Trisha, tell me why the cookie jar is .... *(leer)* again!
10. I was .... *(enttäuscht)* when I got back the test results.
11. The book you gave me was really .... *(aufregend)* to read.

2 ! Put the words into the correct order to form sentences.

EXAMPLE a / tasty / Mum, / chocolate / is / wonderful, / this / cake / !
Mum, this is a wonderful, tasty chocolate cake!

1. at / Yesterday / this / young / saw / the / woman / I / beautiful / shop

   ....

2. Carrie / green / In / handbag / canvas / bought / a / holidays / new / the

   ....

3. remember / saw / the / Do / handsome / you / boy / tall / we / last night / ?

   ....

4. Where / leather / my / boots / black / are / ?

   ....

5. offer / many / E-books / to / English / interesting / the reader / English / novels / in

   ....

C comparison of the adjective – Steigerung und Vergleich

Wenn wir Sachen miteinander vergleichen wollen, brauchen wir dazu das Adjektiv und seine Steigerungsstufen.

Grundstufe *positive*	1. Steigerungsstufe/Mehrstufe *comparative*	2. Steigerungsstufe/Meiststufe *superlative*
large	*larger*	*(the) largest*
fascinating	*more fascinating*	*(the) most fascinating*
good	*better*	*(the) best*

Englische Adjektive bilden die Steigerungsstufen auf drei verschiedene Arten:

C1 Die „einfache" Steigerung mit -(e)r und -(e)st gilt für:

- **einsilbige** Adjektive: cool – cool**er** – cool**est**
- **zweisilbige** Adjektive, die auf **-y** enden: eas**y** – eas**ier** – eas**iest**; happ**y** – happ**ier** – happ**iest**

ACHTUNG RECHTSCHREIBUNG!

- einfacher Konsonant nach einfachem Vokal → **Verdoppelung**
  big – bigger – biggest *fat – fatter – fattest*
- **-y** nach Konsonant → **wird zu -i**
  lazy – lazier – laziest *lucky – luckier – luckiest*
- bei **-e am Wortende** wird nur mehr **-r** und **-st** angehängt
  late – later – latest *nice – nicer – nicest*

C2 ! Die „zusammengesetzte" Steigerung mit *more* und *most* gilt für:

- alle **drei- und mehrsilbigen** Adjektive:
  popular – ***more** popular* – ***most** popular*
  complicated – ***more** complicated* – ***most** complicated*
- alle **zweisilbigen Adjektive**, die **nicht auf -y** enden:
  famous – ***more*** famous – **most** famous
  boring – ***more*** boring – **most** boring

ACHTUNG!

Manche zweisilbige Adjektive steigern **mit *-er/-est* oder mit *more/most*.**

- Adjektive, die auf ***-ow***, ***-er*** und ***-le*** enden:

*narr**ow***		*clev**er***		*simp**le***	
narrower	*more narrow*	*cleverer*	*more clever*	*simpler*	*more simple*
narrowest	*most narrow*	*cleverest*	*most clever*	*simplest*	*most simple*

- die folgenden Adjektive:

common – cruel – handsome – likely – pleasant – polite – quiet – stupid – sure – tired

common		cruel		stupid	
commoner	more common	crueler	more cruel	stupider	more stupid
commonest	most common	cruelest	most cruel	stupidest	most stupid

C3 Die „unregelmäßige" Steigerung gilt für:

positive	comparative	superlative	deutsche Bedeutung
good	*better*	*best*	gut
well			gesund
bad	*worse*	*worst*	schlecht, böse
evil			böse, bösartig
ill			krank
many	*more*	*most*	viele (Zählbares)
much			viel (Nicht-Zählbares)
little	*less*	*least*	wenig (Nicht-Zählbares)
	smaller	*smallest*	klein

C4 ! Unterschiedliche Bedeutung bei den Steigerungsstufen bei:

positive	comparative	superlative	deutsche Bedeutung
late	*later*	*latest*	später (Zeit)
	latter	–	letzterer, letztgenannter
	–	*last*	der letzte (Reihenfolge)
near	*nearer*	*nearest*	nahe/näher/... (Entfernung)
	–	*next*	nächster (Reihenfolge)
far	*farther*	*farthest*	fern, weit (Entfernung)
	further	*furthest*	weitere, zusätzliche
old	*older*	*oldest*	älter / am ältesten
	elder	*eldest*	älter/... (Familienmitglieder)

3 Circle the correct forms.

EXAMPLE Apple produced *good/better* things when Steve Jobs was still alive.

1. Can you tell me where the *next/nearest* underground station is?
2. My best friend Mia did *worse/worst* than me in the last French test.
3. Tim, which of the two girls over there looks *prettier/prettyer*?
4. Which teacher is *more strict/stricter*, Mr Haysmith or Mr Goldbloom?
5. Nobody in my class gets *little/less* pocket money than I do.

4 Decide if you need comparative or superlative.

Dear Josy,

How are you? I haven't heard from you for a long time so I hope everything is alright!

I am writing to tell you about my last winter holidays which were really **more exciting** *(exciting)* than usual. Guess what! I went camping in the Tyrol and it was amazing. We arrived at the campsite ______________ *(late)* than we expected because there was so much snow on the motorway so that the drive simply took ______________ *(long)*. Plus, with a motorhome you can't drive very fast anyway. Upon our arrival I realised that there was an amazing amount of snow – I guess I have never seen ______________ *(much)* snow in my life than in the Tyrol!

Spending the holidays in a motorhome is a lot of fun! Of course you have ______________ *(little)* space than in a hotel room but actually everything is very comfortable. Only taking a shower is ______________ *(hard)* compared to normal because the bathroom is really tiny. But the kitchen is okay and cooking was much ______________ *(easy)* than I thought. The ______________ *(good)* thing, however, was that the motorhome also had a TV set. So we didn't get bored in the evenings. Sleeping was fine although after a few nights my back felt ______________ *(bad)* than at the beginning of the trip. But somehow I didn't mind. All in all I have to say that these were the ______________ *(great)* winter holidays I've ever had!

What about you? Let me know what you were doing and write back soon! Love, Trish!

C5 Vergleiche

X und Y lassen sich auf verschiedene Weise miteinander vergleichen:

(a) X kann **so (lang) wie** Y sein oder **nicht so (lang) wie** Y sein;

(b) X kann **(länger) als** Y sein;

(c) X (oder Y) kann **der/die/das (längste)** sein.

(a) positive	*(b) comparative*	*(c) superlative*
as long (short ...) as *not as long (short ...) as* *not so long (short ...) as*	*longer (shorter ...) than*	*the longest (shortest ...)*
*A yard is **not as long as** a metre.*	*A foot is **shorter than** a yard.*	*A mile is **the longest**.*
*This is **as easy as** it looks.*	*It's **more difficult than** it looks.*	*It's **the easiest / the most difficult** thing to do.*
*Some films are **as good as** a book.*	*Some films are **worse than** a book.*	*This film is **the worst / the best** in a long time.*

C6 !! Der Vergleich mit „je – desto“

Bei dieser Art des Vergleichs verwendet man den bestimmten Artikel (***the***) und die Mehrstufe des Adjektivs (***comparative***).

Je billiger, desto besser.
→ ***The cheaper, the better.***

Je früher du wegfährst, desto früher wirst du hier sein.
→ ***The sooner** you leave, **the sooner** you'll get here.*

Beim Wein ist es so: je älter, desto teurer.
→ *With wine it's like this: **the older, the more expensive**.*

C7 ! Die Steigerung mit „immer“ (zunehmende Steigerung)

Die Musik wurde **immer lauter**.
→ *The music was getting **louder and louder**.*

Die Geschichte wurde **immer langweiliger**.
→ *The story got **more and more boring**.*

- **Wiederholung des *comparative*** → bei Steigerung mit *-er/-est*
  bei unregelmäßiger Steigerung
- **Wiederholung von *more*** → bei Steigerung mit *more/most*

5 !! Translate the following comparisons.

EXAMPLE Ich bin besser in Englisch, meine Freundin ist schlechter in Mathematik.
I'm better at English, my friend is worse at maths.

1. Je eher du es tust, desto besser!

2. Jimmy ist kleiner als Johnny, aber er ist schwerer.

3. Ich finde, *Oblivion* war spannender als *Hanni & Nanni 3*.

4. Während der letzten Englischstunde wurde ich immer müder.

6 ! Decide which adjective is suitable.

March 12th:

After a very ~~tired~~/*tiring* flight I have finally landed in Australia. I can hardly move my body from all the long hours of just sitting, but otherwise I'm fine and very *exciting/excited* about the two week trip to the Outback that lies ahead of me ☺! I'm sure it's going to be *good/bad*!

March 14th:

We have already met our guide and he seems to be rather *friendly/unfriendly*. His name is Obawama and he is Aboriginal. This means he is a *native/naive* Australian and has spent almost all his life in the Outback. We are all terribly *interested/interesting* in the stories he tells us because life here really seems to be *similar/different* to the European way of living.

March 19th:

I have already spent my first few nights in the tent in the Outback and it's simply *amazed/amazing*! Obawama has also shown us some wild animals, but of course we have to be very *careless/careful*. It's *important/unimportant* to watch out for poisonous snakes. Roberta, another member of our group, saw an ugly black snake yesterday and she was really *scary/scared*. But then Obawama told us not to be afraid because it was *harmful/harmless*. That was really *surprising/surprised* as we all thought we were going to die …

I don't know if I'll have Internet access during the next *many/few* days, so I'd better say goodbye now! See you soon back home ☺!

7 !! Find the opposite adjective.

EXAMPLE dead *alive*

1. numerous ____________
2. ____________ uncountable
3. expensive ____________
4. responsible ____________
5. polite ____________
6. rich ____________
7. mature ____________
8. ____________ major
9. ____________ lazy
10. ____________ passive
11. sane ____________

8 !! Complete the sentences with an adjective from above.

EXAMPLE *Poor* developing countries stand in opposition to wealthy, industrial ones.

1. Only ____________ of my friends like unsolved mysteries.
2. Honestly, your new friend is a very ____________ and rude person.
3. Tell me, Frank, are you ____________ for the broken window?
4. Compared with a tsunami, an avalanche is a ____________ disaster.
5. Wow, you really exercise a lot. You're such an ____________ person!
6. She never does anything but is always tired. She's so ____________!
7. I don't believe that ____________ people come back and haunt us.
8. The iPad is too ____________. I haven't got enough money.
9. Susan, the way you behave is really childish and ____________.
10. An ____________ number of people believe in the existence of UFOs.
11. Are you ____________, John? You can't leave the house in shorts when it's snowing outside!

9 !! Banked gap fill: Unsolved Mysteries

You are going to read about unsolved mysteries. Some words (mostly adjectives) are missing from the text. Choose from the list (A–L) the correct word for each gap (1–9). There are two extra words that you should not use. Write your answers in the space provided. The first one (0) has been done for you.

Unsolved Mysteries

Surely, all of us have already heard about strange happenings and mysterious incidents that cannot be logically explained. We have all experienced **(0)** ___ phenomena and the existence of ghosts and UFOs, either via TV, the radio or the Net. But do things like these really exist? Is extraterrestrial life possible? Do dead people return and wander around with us? Can you heal another person just with your good will and your hands? And is it true that a significantly **(1)** ___ number of airplanes disappears in the Bermuda Triangle? Well, the following article will definitely not provide you with **(2)** ___ answers, but it will look at certain topics in more detail.

Let's start with the well-known Bermuda Triangle. This is an area in the ocean between Florida, San Juan and Bermuda that is heavily sailed. It is believed to be **(3)** ___ for the disappearance of numerous ships, boats and airplanes and even today countless pilots and captains are afraid of going near this **(4)** ___ area. The problematic aspect is that there have indeed been many disappearances that cannot be explained by human error, equipment failure or natural disaster. There is quite a significant number of incidents (or should we rather say *accidents*?) that simply lack logic and **(5)** ___ explanations. The first of these unexplained events occurred in the 1950s. Since then stories have been spread telling us that the Bermuda Triangle is a **(6)** ___ zone. Critics, of course, don't believe in all this gossip, and they claim that the Bermuda Triangle is responsible for no more disappearances than any other area of the ocean.

Another frequently discussed phenomenon is extraterrestrial life and whether or not it exists on planet Earth. Extraterrestrial life is life that does not originate from our planet. It is often also referred to as alien life or simply aliens. The number of people who claim to have seen an alien or a spaceship in the middle of a cornfield is most probably quite **(7)** ___, but the interesting thing is that many scientists consider extraterrestrial life to be plausible and possible. Of course, there is no direct evidence, but a lot of speculation and assumptions.

Finally, what about hands-on healing? Is it really possible that another person can heal me just by touching my **(8)** ___ body parts? Well, according to some articles on the Internet it is! It is unbelievable but true – the phenomenon of healing hands can be explained! It goes as follows: healing is all about resonance and vibrations. Healers learn to hold a high vibration in their hands and when they touch another human being, they pass on their high energy to the other person. And that's why the other person feels **(9)** ___. Sounds very simple, doesn't it? It's a pity, though, that not everything in life is so easy!

A	aching	**B**	better	**C**	comprehensible
D	dead	**E**	death	**F**	high
G	indefinite	**H**	legendary	**I**	low
J	precise	**K**	responsible	**L**	*unexplainable*

0	1	2	3	4	5	6	7	8	9
L									

10 !! Word formation: Oprah Winfrey

You are going to read a text about Oprah Winfrey. Some words are missing. Use the words in brackets to complete each gap (1–8) in the text. Mind comparisons. Write your answers in the spaces provided at the end of the text. The first one (0) has been done for you.

Talk Show Queen Faces Racism

Everybody knows and loves Oprah Winfrey, America's richest, **(0)** ______ **(success)** and most popular talk show queen and entertainer. Or at least you would think so. Go on reading and find out more about an embarrassing incident:

It was in August 2013 when the US superstar travelled to Switzerland in order to attend Tina Turner's wedding in Zurich. Days before the **(1)** ______ **(spectacle)** event, Oprah set off for one of her **(2)** ______ **(fame)** and excessive shopping tours that led her to the Trois Pommes luxury boutique. Mesmerised by the **(3)** ______ **(extravagance)** model of a 25,000 £ handbag, Oprah asked the shop assistant to show her the item. This, however, proved to be **(4)** ______ **(difficulty)** than expected, as the young and obviously ignorant sales person refused to do so. After suspiciously eying the black superstar (without identifying her as such), the salesperson tried to get rid of her by saying that she didn't want to hurt Oprah's feelings, as she was sure that Oprah wouldn't be able to afford such an expensive handbag. Keeping her calm, Oprah left the shop stating that the assistant was probably right.

The next day, however, Oprah claimed that she was faced with a **(5)** ______ **(race)** attack, assuming that the young saleswoman had only refused to serve her because of her black skin. On being interviewed on this subject, the owner of the luxury boutique asserted that she would never consider one of her **(6)** ______ **(trust)** employees a racist. She was absolutely convinced that the whole incident must have been due to a simple **(7)** ______ **(language)** misunderstanding. "Believe me, I do feel **(8)** ______ **(desperation)** about this blunder and wish to apologise from the bottom of my heart", says the shop owner. When Oprah learned about the real price of the handbag, she confirmed that she would never have bought such an expensive accessory anyway.

EXAMPLE **0.** *most successful*

1. ______

2. ______

3. ______

4. ______

5. ______

6. ______

7. ______

8. ______

ADJECTIVE (EIGENSCHAFTSWORT)

ÜBEN

ADVERB – UMSTANDSWORT

Das Adverb (Umstandswort) dient zur näheren Beschreibung eines Verbs, eines Adjektives oder eines anderen Adverbs. Manchmal bezieht es sich auf einen ganzen Satz.

Das Adverb gibt an:

- **wie** etwas geschieht → Art und Weise: ***adverbs of manner***
- **wo** etwas geschieht → Ort: ***adverbs of place***
- **wann** etwas geschieht → Zeit: ***adverbs of time***
- **wie oft** etwas geschieht → Häufigkeit: ***adverbs of frequency***
- **wie sehr** etwas geschieht → Grad, Ausmaß: ***adverbs of degree***
- **wie ein ganzer Satz gemeint ist** → Satzadverb: ***sentence adverbials***

A Bildung des Adverbs

Viele Adverbien, vor allem die *adverbs of manner*, werden nach dem folgenden Muster gebildet:

adjective + ly

ACHTUNG RECHTSCHREIBUNG!

„Normalfälle“			
adjective	→ *adverb*	*adjective*	→ *adverb*
clear	→ *clear**ly***	*democratic*	→ *democrat**ically***
perfect	→ *perfect**ly***	*terrific*	→ *terrif**ically***
Ausnahme!			
		public	→ *publ**icly***

„Sonderfälle“					
lucky	→ *luck**ily***	*terrible*	→ *terrib**ly***	*due*	→ *du**ly***
easy	→ *eas**ily***	*simple*	→ *simp**ly***		
Ausnahmen!					
shy	→ *shy**ly***	*dry*	→ *dry**ly***		

manner	*awfully, fast, easily, terribly, well, slowly, perfectly …* *Our team played* ***terribly*** *all season.*	*→ how?*
place	*here, abroad, somewhere, outside, upstairs, indoors, away …* *Nigel lived* ***abroad*** *for a while. – Wait* ***outside!***	*→ where?*
time	*now, then, today, tomorrow, tonight, yesterday, finally, later …* *The show starts* ***now****. – I'll talk to you* ***later****!*	*→ when?*
frequency	*once, twice, daily, weekly, always, often, occasionally, rarely …* *I spoke to Joe only* ***once****. – Jill* ***rarely*** *goes out.*	*→ how often?*
degree	*almost, barely, fairly, hardly, just, quite, rather, too, very …* *This photo is* ***almost*** *perfect. – That's* ***too*** *bad.*	*→ how (bad)?*
sentence adverbials	*actually, (un)fortunately, luckily, accordingly, otherwise …* *A BMW is a great car.* ***Unfortunately****, it's too expensive for me!* *Joe had an accident yesterday.* ***Luckily****, he wasn't hurt.*	

11 Complete the story about Cathy's stay at the Frequency Festival. Use adverb forms of the adjectives in brackets and mind the spelling of the adverb!

EXAMPLE Hi, I'm Cathy and I want to tell you about the exciting experience I had at this year's Frequency Festival in Lower Austria. My boyfriend **surprisingly** invited me to join him at this music festival in the middle of August.

…………………… *(unfortunate)* I had never been to such an event so I felt …………………… *(extreme)* nervous. Days before, I had already started to pack my stuff, but soon realised that I would have to leave half the things behind that I had …………………… *(original)* intended to take with me. So when my boyfriend …………………… *(final)* came to pick me up, I was still carrying an …………………… *(impressive)* huge backpack, and I was …………………… *(real)* irritated when he laughed …………………… *(loud)*. Upon our arrival I felt …………………… *(total)* surprised and overwhelmed: I saw hundreds of tents …………………… *(close)* packed on a muddy and dirty patch of grass. I looked around …………………… *(unbelieving)* and was close to tears. I …………………… *(instinctive)* knew that I would never ever be able to spend four days at that place! I shouted at my boyfriend …………………… *(hysterical)*, but again he …………………… *(simple)* laughed. Grinning …………………… *(wicked)*, he took out two tickets and said, "We are VIP, baby! Don't worry, just relax and enjoy the show!" ☺

B Ausnahmen

1. **Einige Adverbien** werden **nicht durch das Anhängen von -ly** gebildet. Entweder sie gleichen den Adjektiven oder sie sind „Sonderformen".

adjective	*adverb*	Bedeutung	*examples*
good	*well*	gut	*Mary is a very good person.* *Everybody speaks well of her.*
fast	*fast*	schnell, rasch	*My dad always has fast cars.* *He likes driving fast.*
hard	*hard*	hart, schwer	*This has been a hard week for me.* *I've had to work hard every day.*
high	*high*	hoch	*George loves high mountains.* *His house is high in the mountains.*
early	*early*	früh, zeitig	*My father is an "early bird".* *He gets up early every morning.*
late	*late*	spät	*Rick often watches the late news on TV, but he is never late for work next day.*

2. Manche Adjektive auf -ly bilden keine Adverbien. Man verwendet in diesen Fällen die Wendung ***in a (...) way/manner***.

Zu dieser Gruppen zählen zB:
friendly, kindly, lively, lonely, lovely, melancholy, orderly, silly und ***ugly***.
→ *Mark and Judy are* ***lively children****. They do everything* ***in a lively manner****.*

12 Find the correct forms of the adjective or adverb.

	adjective	adverb
1.	sad	*sadly*
2.	tired	
3.	unfriendly	
4.	excited	
5.		well
6.		prettily
7.	horrible	
8.	careful	
9.		badly
10.		high

	adjective	adverb
11.		dully
12.	late	
13.	straight	
14.		wholly
15.	ugly	
16.		responsibly
17.	terrific	
18.	sly	
19.	silly	
20.	happy	

13 ! Name the word in *italic type*: adjective or adverb? Write down the word it refers to.

	sentence	adjective/adverb	word it refers to
1.	We have got an absolutely *crazy* dog.	adjective	dog (noun)
2.	Angelina is a *fast* skier.		
3.	Don't walk so *fast*!		
4.	Don't you think that Steve dances *wonderfully*?		
5.	My girlfriend cooks really *badly*.		
6.	Listen, Pamela sings *beautifully*!		
7.	Isn't that a *pretty* dress, Jill?		
8.	Open the box *slowly* – the snake might escape.		
9.	My Mum worked very *hard* last week.		
10.	Look how *high* our kitty can climb!		
11.	This is a *very* dangerous mountain to climb.		

14 Fill in adjective or adverb.

EXAMPLE Don't shout at me so **angrily**! It wasn't my mistake!

1. Since last year we have had a .... *(strict)* English teacher.
2. During our date Ricardo smiled at me .... *(sweet)*.
3. The number of unemployed teens has risen .... *(dramatic)*.
4. Mum always tells me not to come home .... *(late)*.
5. Johnny, come over here .... *(fast)*, I need your help!
6. "I need you .... *(desperate)*!", cried Mary.
7. This is a really .... *(boring)* exercise, so let's move on!

C ! Verschiedene Bedeutung von Adjektiv und Adverb

Einige *adjectives* haben **zwei** Adverbien, deren Bedeutungen jedoch unterschiedlich sind:

adjective/adverb		*adverb*		*examples*
close	nahe	*closely*	genau	*I live close to the city centre.* *The dog watched us closely.*
deep	tief	*deeply*	zutiefst	*These are deep waters indeed!* *I'm deeply thankful to you all.*
direct	direkt	*directly*	gleich, sofort	*Let's take the direct approach.* *Let's go directly to the boss!*
free	frei, gratis	*freely*	freimütig, ohne Scheu	*Can you get free tickets?* *You can speak freely here!*
full	voll	*fully*	völlig	*The boat is full.* *I fully realise my mistake.*
hard	hart, schwer	*hardly*	kaum	*We worked hard all day.* *We hardly slept all night.*
high	hoch	*highly*	höchst, sehr	*I'm shocked at the high prices.* *This is highly irregular!*
late	spät	*lately*	vor kurzem, unlängst	*Christmas is late in the year.* *You look tired lately!*
most	(meist)	*mostly*	hauptsächlich	*Most people have hobbies.* *She talked mostly about music.*
near	nahe	*nearly*	beinahe, fast	*We could smell the near sea.* *I nearly had an accident today.*

D ! Verben, auf die kein Adverb folgt

Auf bestimmte Verben folgt das Adjektiv und nicht das Adverb. Diese Verben beschreiben **keine Handlungen, sondern Zustände**.

- Alle Formen von **to be**: *Austrians **are good** at skiing.*
  *The summer holidays **will be wonderful**.*
  *This year **has been perfect** so far.*
- Die Verben ***feel, look, smell, seem, sound*** und ***taste***, wenn sie einen **Zustand** beschreiben:
  *Julia **feels nervous** before a play.*
  *Lena **looks strange** with her new haircut.*
  *Your socks **smell terrible**, Mike! Wash them!*
  *The new songs **sound great**! I love them.*
  *Dinner at "El Gaucho" **tasted fantastic**.*

  ABER → Adverb, wenn das Verb eine **Handlung** beschreibt:
  *Julia **felt nervously** for my hand before the play.* → Handlung
  *Lena **looked** at me **strangely**, but I had no idea why.* → Handlung
  *Troy **smelled** the cheese **thoroughly** before trying it.* → Handlung
  *The chef **tasted** the sauce **carefully** before serving it.* → Handlung
- Die Verben ***become, get, go, grow*** und ***turn***, wenn sie „werden" bedeuten:
  *The crowd **became angry** when the concert was cancelled.*
  *A good teacher doesn't **get nervous** easily.*
  *I'll **go crazy** if this **noise** doesn't stop at once!*
  *The coffee **turned cold** before we could drink it.*

15 Circle the correct form.

EXAMPLE This is an *extreme/extremely* cool car. It can go very *fast/fastly*.

1. That cake tastes so *good/well*. Your mum is a *wonderful/wonderfully* cook.
2. Why have you done so *bad/badly* in your last maths test, Pete?
3. That's Cleo over there. She always works so *hard/hardly* – I wonder if she ever has fun.
4. I spent a *totally/total* awesome evening with the girl I went out with yesterday.
5. Believe me, Barney *truly/truely* loves you.
6. There is fog everywhere, I can *hard/hardly* see anything at all.
7. I'm so angry. I've just found out I'll earn *fewer/less* money than last summer.
8. This street is *wholy/wholly* owned by Mr Rockefeller. Imagine that!
9. The Parker sisters really resemble each other *close/closely*.

16 ! Adjective or adverb? Fill in the correct form of the words in brackets.

EXAMPLE When I was driving home from school yesterday afternoon, a truck came ***dangerously*** close to my car.

1. Anna Netrebko has just released a .... *(wonderful)* new CD.
2. Don't look so .... *(angry)*. What's the matter?
3. Why is Ms Simpson looking at me so .... *(angry)*?
4. When you have a dog, you have to act very .... *(responsible)*.
5. Who is talking so .... *(loud)*? I wonder why it is always so .... *(noisy)* in this class.
6. Annabelle is a .... *(good)* dancer but she doesn't sing very .... *(good)*.
7. Don't come .... *(near)* the dog. It bites.
8. I .... *(near)* failed my maths test. I got 26 points out of 50.
9. Why did you insult me so .... *(terrible)*?
10. Sandra! Go .... *(straight)* to the headmaster!
11. Look how .... *(nice)* decorated this room is.
12. The Killers always give a .... *(strong)* performance.

17 ! **Complete the text with a suitable word.**

Hi Jenna,

The reason why I am writing to you is **quite/rather** *(ziemlich)* urgent. I know I can talk ________________ *(offen)* to you. Read ________________ *(aufmerksam)* and think ________________ *(sorgfältig)* – I need some ________________ *(gut)* advice.

Two weeks ago, Steve, the boy I've had a ________________ *(groß)* crush on for months, asked me to go to The Killers concert with him the following Saturday. I felt so ________________ *(aufgeregt)* I could ________________ *(kaum)* sleep all week. When at last the doorbell rang, I felt ________________ *(ziemlich)* nervous and my heart was beating so ________________ *(schnell)* I thought it would burst. I opened the door ________________ *(langsam)* and there he was: Steve – looking ________________ *(großartig)* and smiling ________________ *(süß)*. He drove me ________________ *(sicher)* to the concert and we enjoyed a ________________ *(fantastisch)* show. The Killers played their ________________ *(neueste)* album and we had an ________________ *(unglaublich)* great time. After the show, Steve drove me home ________________ *(sofort)* because my stupid parents had told him to do so. When we were standing outside my door, he looked ________________ *(tief)* into my eyes. He came closer and closer and finally he kissed me ________________ *(sanft)* on my lips. And guess what – at that moment my parents opened the door and looked at us, ________________ *(zutiefst)* shocked. I couldn't even say goodbye to Steve but had to go to my room at once. Then my mum had a very long talk with me. She seemed ________________ *(wahrlich)* hurt and warned me against becoming too intimate with a boy and getting pregnant and so on. I was so ________________ *(überrascht)* I started to laugh! Of course, that didn't help a lot. So now I'm grounded until 2045, I guess. Jenna, I'm totally ________________ *(verzweifelt)*. How I can make things right again with my parents? I'm looking forward to your reply.

Love, Tina

18 !! Translate the sentences.

EXAMPLE Ich war ziemlich gut bei der letzten Englischschularbeit.
I did quite well at the last English test.

1. Oh nein! Du bist beinahe hingefallen.

2. Komm Patrick nicht zu nahe! Er hat einen schlimmen Schnupfen.

3. Hör genau zu!

4. Spielt fair, aber gewinnt!

5. Ich schlief letzte Woche kaum.

E Steigerung des Adverbs *(comparison of the adverb)*

So wie das Adjektiv lässt sich auch das Adverb steigern:

Wie?	Was?	Zum Beispiel:
more und ***most***	alle Adverbien, die sich durch das Anhängen von **-ly** aus einem Adjektiv ableiten lassen	*strongly – more strongly – most strongly* *thorough – more thoroughly – most thoroughly*
-(e)r und **-(e)st**	alle Adverbien, die sich **nicht** durch Anhängen von **-ly** aus einem Adjektiv ableiten lassen	*hard – harder – hardest* *high – higher – highest* *early – earlier – earliest*
unregelmäßig	*well*	*well – better – best*
	badly	*badly – worse – worst*
	little (wenig)	*little – less – least*

19 ! Complete with the correct comparison.

EXAMPLE This year I'm earning even less *(weniger)* than last year.

1. Rick, you have to pull ________ *(stärker/fester)*!
2. Sorry, Sir, but today I have to leave ________ *(früher)*.
3. Unfortunately, Nora did ________ *(schlechter)* than me again.

20 !! Multiple choice: Another Celebrity Divorce

You are going to read a text about Hollywood actor Tom Cruise. Some words are missing from the text. Choose the correct answer (A, B, C or D) for each gap (1–10). Then write your answers in the space provided. The first one (0) has been done for you.

Another Celebrity Divorce

Everybody knows him and many among us **(0)** ______ admire and love him: top Hollywood actor Tom Cruise. Originally born Thomas Cruise Mapother in 1962, he has featured in numerous **(1)** ______ known movies (like *Jerry Maguire*, *Top Gun* or *Minority Report*), but is probably most famous for his *Mission Impossible* action films. In these he plays secret agent Ethan Hunt, who fights against bad and evil, is involved in **(2)** ______ life-threatening incidents but somehow **(3)** ______ always manages to survive. Therefore it's no surprise that Cruise is said to be Hollywood's **(4)** ______ paid actor.

Tom Cruise has constantly been in the media, either because of his artistic successes or because of his private life, which **(5)** ______ focuses on the so-called Church of Scientology. When taking a closer look at Tom Cruise's private life, it might be worth mentioning that the actor has been married three times. While his first marriage only survived a few short years, his second marriage to actress Nicole Kidman lasted much longer duration but it also ended in divorce. He then **(6)** ______ to marry actress Katie Holmes, whose Hollywood career had basically started with the teen series *Dawsons Creek*. Their wedding, which took place in 2006, might have come as a surprise to some people because the couple appeared to be so different. But they were obviously happy with each other, at least in the beginning. However, their **(7)** ______ life only lasted for about six years, as they, too, got divorced in 2012.

Of course, the media covered this event in great detail and there were stories in almost every paper. According to these, it was Katie's wish to **(8)** ______ up as she could no longer stand her life with Tom. It was reported that she wanted nothing from Tom, other than the divorce. And that was exactly what Katie got: she did not get any spousal support, only rather modest child maintainance for their daughter Suri. But of course the word *modest* has a **(9)** ______ different meaning when it comes to Hollywood, because Tom Cruise pays his ex-wife $ 400,000 a year in child support, which comes down to $ 33,333 a month. So Katie and daughter Suri will obviously not suffer from **(10)** ______ financial problems. Luckily, Tom and Katie agreed on a quick settlement, so as not to strain Suri's emotional state unnecessarily. The way it seems, it has been the fastest celebrity divorce ever.

0	A	terribly	B	terribely	C	**truly**	D	truely
1	A	good	B	well	C	badly	D	moderately
2	A	uncountable	B	uncountably	C	unaccounted	D	unaccountedly
3	A	mysteriousely	B	mysterious	C	mystery	D	mysteriously
4	A	high	B	higher	C	highly	D	highest
5	A	stronger	B	strongly	C	strangely	D	strictly
6	A	ordered	B	organised	C	opted	D	offered
7	A	harmonious	B	harmoniously	C	harmony	D	harmonically
8	A	turn	B	quit	C	come	D	split
9	A	complete	B	completely	C	completly	D	constantly
10	A	severer	B	severely	C	severly	D	severe

0	1	2	3	4	5	6	7	8	9	10
C										

21 !! Banked gap fill: 2012 Summer Paralympic Games

You are going to read a text about the 2012 Paralympic Games in London. Some words are missing from the text. Choose from the list (A–P) the correct word for each gap (1–13) in the text. There are two extra words that you should not use. Write your answers in the space provided. The first one (0) has been done for you.

2012 Summer Paralympic Games

Between August 29th and September 9th, 2012, the Summer Paralympic Games were **(0)** .... for the 14th time, the hosting city being London, similar to the Summer Olympic Games. The interest in and fascination with the Paralympics was as big as had been expected, and **(1)** .... to the event it was **(2)** .... that over 4,200 athletes from 164 nations would participate and **(3)** .... against one another. By the way, the first sports event for disabled people was held **(4)** .... after World War II, also in England, in a village called Stoke Mandeville. Those games served as a precursor to the modern Paralympic Games.

The Summer Paralympics **(5)** .... used the same venues and infrastructure as the 2012 Summer Olympics. **(6)** .... some things had to be adapted for the changed circumstances, like the venues for wheelchair tennis and road cycling. In the Olympic village itself, however, the changes were **(7)** .... as it had been constructed in a way to accommodate **(8)** .... handicapped athletes as well. Houses and apartments had been designed to host people unable to walk and this, of course, saved a lot of money afterwards as it made elaborate construction work **(9)** ....

A growing interest in Paralympic sport worldwide, as well as Great Britain's success during the recent Summer Olympics, helped to raise the demand for the tickets **(10)** .... All in all, about 2.5 million tickets were made available before the official start of the Games, and almost all of these tickets (about 2.4 million) were sold by August 28th. And it's no wonder, because people **(11)** .... love to see first class elite sports. It doesn't matter that the athletes are handicapped, sit in wheelchairs or suffer from some sort of deformity. On the contrary, these people must be admired, adored and looked up to because they are **(12)** .... and most probably also physically much stronger than people like you and me. They have managed something that is unbelieveable and have overcome their personal limitations, fears and prejudices. Taking part in the Paralympic Games, and maybe even winning a medal, **(13)** .... does not only mean the highlight of their sports careers, but also of their personal and private lives.

Last but not least: while the Summer Olympic Games were not very successful from an Austrian point of view, as no medals at all were won, Austrian Paralympic athletes were extremely successful and took home several gold, silver and bronze medals.

A	basically	B	compete	C	estimated	D	hardly
E	*held*	F	mentally	G	minor	H	necessary
I	physically	J	presumably	K	prior	L	shortly
M	significantly	N	simply	O	surely	P	unnecessary

0	1	2	3	4	5	6	7	8	9	10	11	12	13
E													

22 !! Word formation: Facebook and Other Threats

You are going to read a text about possible dangers related to Facebook and other social media. Some words are missing from the text. Use the correct form of the words in brackets to complete each gap (1–18) in the text. Write your answers in the spaces provided at the end of the text. The first one (0) has been done for you.

Facebook and Other Threats

Do the words *social media* ring a bell? And have you ever asked **(0)** ______ **(you)** what YOU have got to do with it? No? Well, here we go with the answers:

To start with, social media technologies can take on many different forms and might **(1)** ______ **(appearance)** to be Internet forums, weblogs, social blogs (like *Twitter*), wikis, social networks or podcasts. Of the terms just mentioned, "social networks" is probably the best known as it includes Internet sites like *Facebook*, *Bebo* or *MySpace*. And who doesn't know these? *Facebook* is definitely the most popular and most widely used site. **(2)** ______ **(foundation)** by Mark Zuckerberg some time after the millennium, it has now about 955 million users, the number **(3)** ______ **(constant)** rising. No doubt, *Facebook* offers many possibilities and creates **(4)** ______ **(imaginable)** advantages but sadly, especially teenagers don't realise that a *Facebook* account might also bear considerable **(5)** ______ **(risky)**.

These days, the average *Facebook* user gets younger and younger. They **(6)** ______ **(compilation)** an account on their own by giving themselves a creative user name and then reveal lots and lots of personal information. They post addresses, private details and information related to their families. Unfortunately, they remain ignorant until an adult introduces them to the dangers, risks and threats all this might include. They give away so much private information without even knowing it, and even though they press the "delete" button later, their data is still **(7)** ______ **(storage)** and still available. For sure, at such a young age most users are **(8)** ______ **(simple)** too naïve and too trustful for a thing like *Facebook*.

Furthermore, especially children and teenagers don't know how to express themselves **(9)** ______ **(correct)** when typing messages on *Facebook*. They don't think about how their messages might be perceived and that other people might interpret their messages **(10)** ______ **(different)** than they themselves do. This has **(11)** ______ **(repeat)** been proven by the fact that young *Facebook* users formulate an online invitation to a party, for example, but forget to send this information to just a **(12)** ______ **(selection)** group of users. Instead, hundreds of unknown people, strangers in fact, read the message, look forward to the invitation and suddenly appear at the house, confused as to why they are not welcome. A situation like this has led more than once to trouble and the **(13)** ______ **(involve)** of the police.

Another aspect worth considering **(14)** ______ **(critic)** is the fact that young people forget how to communicate with each other in real life. They spend most of their time in front of their PC screens, chatting with mates, posting messages or up/downloading pictures. It seems, they can no longer go out and meet their friends in the park or go biking with them. Everybody appears to be **(15)** ______ **(isolation)** while being in contact with the rest of the world. The sad side effect is that despite this, nobody seems to *really* communicate and to interact any more. It's like being a loner while still being connected online with the rest of the world.

So what can be done about this critical situation? Or should everything be left the way it is? Definitely not! Ideally, parents should show their children how to use the Internet and social media sites like *Facebook* **(16)** ______ **(responsibility)** and sensibly. Online profiles should be created together with an adult who might give reasonable advice while, at the same time, taking the young persons' interests seriously.

To summarise, young users must be made aware of the possible dangers because they simply don't know. They must be told why certain types of information should remain private while others are completely safe. They must learn how to use the Internet responsibly and how to interact **(17)** ______ **(meaning)**. But simultaneously they must be taught that the world outside is still more interesting and more exciting than any virtual world **(18)** ______ **(offer)** online. They should be convinced of the fact that it's definitely worth turning off the computer and going outside to simply enjoy and experience the great outdoors. And every parent's aim should be to find a good compromise between their child's needs and interests and "real" life because it's certainly not the smartest thing to simply forbid the use of the Internet or to block sites like *Facebook*.

0. *yourself*

1. ______________________

2. ______________________

3. ______________________

4. ______________________

5. ______________________

6. ______________________

7. ______________________

8. ______________________

9. ______________________

10. ______________________

11. ______________________

12. ______________________

13. ______________________

14. ______________________

15. ______________________

16. ______________________

17. ______________________

18. ______________________

CONDITIONAL CLAUSES – BEDINGUNGSSÄTZE

A Grundsätzliches über Bedingungen

- Ein Bedingungssatz (*conditional clause*) besteht immer aus **zwei Teilen** – dem **„wenn-Teil"** (der eigentlichen Bedingung) und dem **„dann-Teil"** (der Folge, die eintritt, wenn die Bedingung erfüllt wird).

  Dabei ist die **Bedingung** ein Gliedsatz, der meist mit ***if*** eingeleitet wird; die Folge ist ein Hauptsatz. Die Reihenfolge kann „Bedingung → Folge" oder „Folge → Bedingung" sein.

  Du verwendest ***if*** in der Bedeutung von „falls" und ***when*** in der zeitlichen Bedeutung von „wenn dann".

Bedingung → Folge	Folge → Bedingung
If/When *it rains, the streets are wet.*	*The streets are wet* ***when/if*** *it rains.*
If *you help me, I will help you.*	*I will help you* ***if*** *you help me.*
If *I were you, I would go now.*	*I would go now* ***if*** *I were you.*
If *Joe had been there, you would have seen him.*	*You would have seen Joe* ***if*** *he had been there.*
If *we had won the finals, we would be the new champs.*	*We would be the new champs* ***if*** *we had won the finals.*
mit Beistrich	**ohne Beistrich**

Es gibt **vier Stufen von Bedingungen**, je nachdem, wie sicher oder wahrscheinlich es ist, dass die Folge auch eintritt. Alle vier verlangen ein ganz **bestimmtes Zusammenwirken der Zeiten**:

B ZERO CONDITIONAL – „Die Wahrheit"

Sie gilt für Tatsachenbehauptungen und allgemeine Wahrheiten. Die Bedingung kann mit **„*if*" (*falls*) oder „*when*" (*wenn dann*)** eingeleitet werden.

If/When *Susan* **is** *really sad,*		*nothing* **can** *cheer her up.*
If/When *the temperature* ***reaches*** *100°,*		***water*** *boils.*
Bedingung = ***present tense***	→	Folge = ***present tense***

C FIRST CONDITIONAL – Der „Fall der Wirklichkeit"

Wenn die Bedingung in einer bestimmten Situation erfüllt wird, dann tritt die Folge auch **wirklich** ein.

If *I* **see** *Susan,*		I **will tell** her about your visit.
If *you* **don't** *hurry,*		*we* ***won't catch*** *the train.*
Bedingung = ***present tense***	→	Folge = ***future with will***

23 Build *zero conditional* sentences.

EXAMPLE you – not feed – the dog – it – be – hungry
If/When you don't feed the dog, it is hungry.

1. ice cream – melt – you – leave – it – in the sun

2. oil – swim – on water – you – pour – it – in?

3. Oliver – have – a bad dream – he – not feel – good – the whole day

24 Build *first conditional* sentences.

EXAMPLE Alex – forget – again – to call – Tina – she – be – angry
If Alex forgets again to call Tina, she will be angry.

1. I – not accept – another apology – Mary – lie – to me – one more time

2. Mona – not want – to have – pizza – we – grab – a burger – instead

3. you – have – another drink – I – get – you – one?

4. Dad – not feed – our dog – in the morning – she – bark – the whole day

25 ! *Zero or first conditional?*

1. When my cat *feels* (*feel*) thirsty, it ………… (*drink*) milk.
2. Polly ………… (*not catch*) the train if she ………… ………… (*not hurry up*) now.
3. ………… (*you, buy*) that cute dress if it ………… (*be*) still in the shop?
4. If I ………… (*not exercise*) enough every day, I ………… (*feel*) bad.

D SECOND CONDITIONAL – Der „Fall der Möglichkeit"

Wenn die Bedingung erfüllt wird, dann tritt die Folge **möglicherweise** (aber nicht sicher) ein.

*If I **had** more money,*	*I **wouldn't stay** in this ruin.*
*If we **left** early in the morning,*	*we **would get** there by evening.*
*If Mr Jones **were** a little nicer,*	*everybody **would like** him.*
Bedingung = *past tense* →	**Folge** = *would + verb in base form*

ACHTUNG!

- Bei ***to be*** gilt:

für „gehobenes" Englisch (zB für Geschriebenes)	für die Umgangssprache
*If I **were** in your position, I would …* *If Bob **were** here, we would …* *If it **weren't** so late, you could …*	*If I **was** in your position, I would …* *If Bob **was** here, we would …* *If it **wasn't** so late, you could …*
alle Personen → ***were*** (wird erwartet)	alle Personen → ***was*** (ist möglich)

- **Anstatt** ***would*** ist auch ***could*** möglich:
  *If it weren't so late, you **could** stay a little longer.*

E ! THIRD CONDITIONAL – Der „Fall der Unmöglichkeit"

Die Bedingung kann nicht mehr erfüllt werden, weil der Zeitpunkt dafür schon vorbei ist. Daher ist es **unmöglich** geworden, dass die Folge eintritt.

*If I **had studied** for the test,*	*I **would have passed** it.*
*If you **hadn't fallen** asleep,*	*you **would have heard** the story.*
*If Marcia **had been** late,*	*we **wouldn't have waited** for her.*
Bedingung = *past perfect tense* →	**Folge** = *would have + 3rd form*

Wenn eine Bedingung nicht erfüllt wurde und auch nicht mehr erfüllt werden kann, weil der Zeitpunkt dafür schon vorbei ist, kann das Auswirkungen auf das „Hier und Jetzt" haben.

*If I **had said** sorry,*	*my friends **wouldn't be** so angry now.*
*If you **had come** in time,*	*we **could go** to the cinema now.*
*If Mike **hadn't warned** me,*	*I **would be** in serious trouble now.*
Bedingung = *past perfect tense* → (kann nicht mehr erfüllt werden)	**Folge** = *would + verb in base form* (wirkt sich *now* aus)

26 Second conditional – Complete the sentences.

1. If Frankie **had** *(have)* a dog, he .... *(take)* it for a walk three times a day.
2. I .... *(not eat)* that sandwich if I .... *(be)* you. It's two days old.
3. If you .... *(not work)* so hard, you .... *(enjoy)* your life more.
4. What .... *(you, do)* if you .... *(win)* the lottery?
5. .... *(Paul, eat)* so much pork if he .... *(know)* how much the poor pigs had to suffer?

27 ! Third conditional – Complete the sentences.

1. If Tanja **had denied** *(deny)* stealing the Blu-ray Disc, she .... *(get)* a much less favourable verdict.
2. You .... *(not blame)* Angela for cheating on her boyfriend now if you .... *(hear)* about what he had done to her.
3. Do you think that Mary .... *(confide)* her secret to Nico if she .... *(know)* that Nico was such a chatterbox?
4. Steve, you .... *(know)* the answer to my question if you .... *(read)* the book, as I told you.
5. .... *(you, purchase)* your car if you .... *(be)* informed about its high petrol consumption?
6. We .... *(not sit)* here now in that broken-down car if you .... *(take)* it to the mechanic when I told you!

28 ! Mixed conditionals – Tick the correct sentences ✓. Correct the wrong ones. Do not change more than one word.

EXAMPLE ☐ If I am older, I will live in a mansion in L.A.
When I am older, I will live in a mansion in L.A.

1. ☐ I could buy that cool car I saw last month if I have more money.

   ....

2. ☐ If Rihanna had known that thousands of people would storm the train stations, she wouldn't have posted a photo of her arrival time on facebook.

   ....

3. ☐ Will you move to the USA if you ever had the chance to?

   ....

4. ☐ Steve would read more when he had the time.

   ....

29 ! Mixed conditionals – Complete the sentences.

1. If you **leave** *(leave)* wine stains in the sun, they .... *(fade)*.
2. Perhaps Jennifer Lopez .... *(not be)* famous now if she .... *(not date)* P. Diddy years ago.
3. If Jackie .... *(speak)* better English, she .... *(get)* better job offers. Unfortunately her English is disastrous.
4. .... *(you, go)* skiing with me this Sunday if the weather .... *(stay)* fine? I mean, the weather forecast is quite optimistic. ☺
5. I .... *(can, help)* you if you .... *(ask)* me. Why don't you ever ask? Now it's too late.
6. If Bernie .... *(must, pay)* more for the holiday, he .... *(not come)* with us. Fortunately he could afford it and we had loads of fun in Spain.

30 !! Mixed conditionals – Write conditional sentences.

EXAMPLE Mark is not very rich. So, he can only buy a cheap ring for Melissa.
If Mark **had more** money, he ***would buy*** a more precious ring.

1. Oh no, the train leaves in two minutes. Let's run! I think we will make it.

If we ______________ faster, we ______________ the train.

2. I'm sorry. I can't bake that strawberry cake you asked for because you forgot to buy strawberries!

If you ______________ to buy them, I ______________ the cake now.

3. It's a shame that the banking system in Austria is so unfair. Some people think that this is the reason why so many people are poor.

Some people think that if the banking system in Austria ______________ fairer, fewer people ______________ so poor.

4. Angelica can't take too much wine. Every time she has a glass too much, she talks and talks and talks.

When Angelica ______________ too much wine, she ______________ very chatty.

5. I was offered my dream job and so I accepted it.

Who ______________ *(not)* such a great offer if they ______________ the chance to?

6. Cathy is thinking of inviting Tim to her party. Tim would love to go to her party.

If Cathy ______________ Tim to her party, he ______________ yes.

7. Max loves baking cakes, but he never has the time to do so.

What kind of cakes ______________ if he ______________ the time for it?

31 !! Banked gap fill: Driving Instructions for Foreign Countries

You are going to read a guideline about what to do when you drive a car in a foreign country. Some words are missing from the text. Choose from the list (A–L) the correct word for each gap (1–9) in the text. There are two extra words that you should not use. Write your answers in the space provided. The first one (0) has been done for you.

Driving Instructions for Foreign Countries

Every year, especially at the beginning of the summer holidays, thousands of tourists pack their suitcases, **(0)** ____ their cars and travel somewhere abroad. Despite the financial crisis and the urge to save money, travelling and going on holiday is still very popular. But as flying somewhere has become a real financial **(1)** ____, more and more holiday-makers decide to take the car. Sure, it can also be expensive, but going by car makes you far more flexible and you can plan your holiday more individually. However, especially when your trip is not fully organised for you by a travel agency, you have to think about and prepare certain things independently. But even though driving is basically the same wherever you are in the world, going to a foreign country by car **(2)** ____ some thought and research. Why? Well, in order to ensure your personal safety and comfort.

Step 1: **(3)** ____ yourself with the way people drive in the **(4)** ____ country you have chosen as your holiday destination. That means checking out if people drive, for example, on the other side of the road, as is the case in the United Kingdom. In addition, acquire a full copy of the Highway Code of the country you want to visit, as well as a comprehensive book of rules governing driving, and be sure to consider typical and local customs and to act accordingly. If you don't want to **(5)** ____ with a roadmap, make sure that your GPS is updated!

Step 2: Memorise fundamental differences between driving laws at home and at your holiday destination. Similarly, memorise differences concerning road **(6)** ____ and their meanings. While the meaning of some signs is quite obvious (like "stop" or "reduce speed"), others might be cryptic and difficult to interpret.

Step 3: Next, find out about the different speed limits. How fast are you allowed to drive on the motorway, on country roads and within cities? **(7)** ____ to these limits by all means because if not, you risk paying high fines and this might easily ruin your good holiday mood. The same holds true for parking. Always check if you need a parking ticket or not, as in the worst case your car will be towed.

Step 4: Finally, don't forget to take your driver's **(8)** ____ because otherwise you will encounter a serious problem. You won't be permitted to drive and the rules are strict as far as this is concerned. Moreover, check your car insurance policy to see if it covers a possible car **(9)** ____ at the respective holiday destination. Last but not least: never drive when you are tired or drunk. Take your time and make breaks whenever you need them. Always remember that you are on holiday and that you should, in fact, relax!

A	burden	B	confirms	C	cruise
D	familiarise	E	licence	F	load
G	navigate	H	rental	I	requires
J	respective	K	signs	L	stick

0	1	2	3	4	5	6	7	8	9
F									

32 ! Follow-up task: Complete the sentences to form correct conditionals.

EXAMPLE If flights *weren't* *(nicht sein)* so expensive, more people would travel this way as it's very comfortable.

1. You .... *(sein)* more flexible and independent if you decide to travel to your holiday destination by car.
2. If you .... *(buchen)* last year's holiday with a travel agency, you would have saved yourself a lot of organisational work.
3. You .... *(müssen)* follow certain guidelines if you want to ensure your safety and comfort while travelling by car.
4. When people .... *(fahren)* on the other side of the road, you have to concentrate more in the beginning.
5. If you had acquired a full copy of the Highway Code of this country, you .... *(nicht haben)* any problems now.

33 !! Follow-up task: Translate the conditionals.

EXAMPLE Wenn du in ein anderes Land reist, wirst du dich informieren müssen
If you travel to another country, you (will) have to inform yourself.

1. Wenn ich mich an die Geschwindigkeitsbegrenzung gehalten hätte, hätte ich keine Strafe (= *fine*) zahlen müssen.

....

....

2. Du hast ein ernsthaftes Problem, wenn dein Auto nicht versichert ist.

....

3. Ich wüsste nicht, was zu tun wäre, wenn ich ein unbekanntes Straßenschild sähe.

....

....

4. Wenn du ein Auto mieten möchtest, musst du mindestens 21 Jahre alt sein.

....

....

34 !! Mixed conditionals.

Read Stefanie's email about a language trip to Saint Malo. Complete the sentences with the correct conditional forms.

Hi Julie,

Thank you for your last email. If I **had known** *(know)* that your parents wanted to spend a week in Vienna, I ____________________ *(invite)* them to stay at our place. So, how did they like their stay? And promise me, when they ________________ *(come)* again, they ________________________ *(must stay)* with us – and you should really join them. ☺

But let me tell you why I am writing to you. I've just returned from my trip to France. We stayed in Saint Malo for five days and then went to Paris for two days. In Saint Malo I stayed with a really nice host family. When I arrived, my host mum said, "Si tu désires quelquechose je t'aiderai bien sûr." That means, "If you ________________ *(need)* something I ________________ *(help)* you." That's nice, isn't it? The first afternoon, we went to the beach. You see, before we left, I had checked the weather forecast, and it predicted a lot of rain. But then, on the second day, the sun came out and I had to buy a bikini. If I ________________ *(know)* what the weather ________________ *(be)* like, I ______________________ *(bring)* that super cool bikini we bought together last year. On the other hand, shopping in France wasn't bad. Anyways, I was lying on the beach when I saw a cute boy approaching me. Of course, I looked great in my new outfit, so we chatted for a while and then we went for a swim. In fact, I found out that this boy was from my area. And now we're a couple! You see, if I ______________________ *(not buy)* that bikini, I __________________________ *(not fall)* in love!

Right, I have to go now. But when I ________________ *(have)* more time, I ________________ *(tell)* you more – I promise!

Hugs and kisses, Stefanie

35 !! Mixed conditionals.

Complete the dialogue with the correct conditional forms of the verbs in brackets.

Robert: Hi Mum! How is it going with your new iPhone?

Sabine: Horribly! It's a disaster. If I ***had been aware*** *(be aware)* that those smartphones are such a mess, I ________ *(stick)* to my old Nokia cell phone.

Robert: Come on, Mum! You can't be serious. If I ________ *(can have)* that phone I ________ *(be)* the happiest person in the world.

Sabine: So you would! But don't be smart now! Help me instead!

Robert: Okay. Look, Mum. If you want to ________ *(send)* a photo, you just ________ *(must)* click here and add the photo.

Sabine: I see – of course, now it works! But I'm sure that if I ________ *(try)* it alone, it ________ *(not work)*.

Robert: What kind of attitude is that? Remember when you helped me with my maths homework and I said the same thing? I also felt like I ________ ________ *(never make)* it if you ________ *(not help)* me. And then you told me to try the next exercise by myself – and I did it! If you ________ ________ *(not give)* me a chance, I ________ ________ *(never see)* how easy it actually was.

Sabine: You're right. Okay. So tell me, what ________ *(happen)* when I ________ *(push)* this button?

Robert: You must remember this – you are talking about the home button here. Every time you ________ *(press)* it, your screen ________ *(return)* to your home menu.

Sabine: Thanks Rob. But hurry up now! See you in the afternoon.

GERUND

A Grundsätzliches über das *gerund*

- Das *gerund* ist eine **ing-form**.
- Das *gerund* ist **das hauptwörtlich gebrauchte Zeitwort** – ein Verb (Zeitwort), das wie ein Nomen (Hauptwort) verwendet wird.

B Formen des *gerund*

	active	*passive*
present	*taking*	*being taken*
perfect	*having taken*	*having been taken*

C Verwendung des *gerund*

- **als Subjekt oder Objekt**, mit oder ohne Artikel:
  subject: ***Travelling*** *broadens the mind.*
  The howling *of the wolves at night was fascinating.*
  object: *I hate* ***tidying*** *up my room every week.*
  All night, we could hear ***the crashing*** *of the waves.*

- **mit oder ohne Präposition** → **verschiedene Bedeutung!**

Can you imagine ***living*** *here?* (Kannst du dir vorstellen, hier zu leben?)	≠	*Can you imagine* ***him/his living*** *here?* (… vorstellen, dass er hier lebt?)
She doesn't mind ***staying*** *here.* (Es macht ihr nichts aus zu bleiben.)	≠	*She doesn't mind* ***us/our staying*** *here.* (Es stört sie nicht, wenn **wir** bleiben.)
We are not used to ***cooking*** *our own meals.* (Wir sind es nicht gewöhnt, uns das Essen selbst zu kochen.)	≠	*We are not used to* ***you/your cooking*** *our meals.* (Wir sind es nicht gewöhnt, dass **ihr** uns das Essen kocht.)

D ! Verben, die zwingend *gerund* verlangen

acknowledge	anerkennen	*excuse*	entschuldigen	*pardon*	entschuldigen
admit	zugeben	*fancy*	gern haben	*postpone*	verschieben
anticipate	erwarten	*finish*	beenden	*practise*	üben
appreciate	würdigen	*forbid*	verbieten	*prevent*	(ver)hindern
avoid	vermeiden	*forgive*	vergeben	*recollect*	erinnern
can't help	nicht anders können	*imagine*	vorstellen	*recommend*	empfehlen
		involve	beinhalten	*resent*	übel nehmen
complete	beenden	*justify*	rechtfertigen	*resist*	widerstehen
consider	bedenken	*keep*	weitermachen	*risk*	riskieren
delay	verzögern	*mention*	erwähnen	*sanction*	billigen
deny	leugnen	*mind*	stören, ausmachen	*suggest*	vorschlagen
discuss	besprechen			*tolerate*	ertragen
enjoy	genießen	*miss*	vermissen	*understand*	verstehen

36 ! Complete the sentences with gerund forms. Mind active and passive forms, as well as present and past forms.

EXAMPLE Singing *(sing)* is one of my favourite hobbies.

1. I remember ________________ *(see)* this film last year.
2. Most people think that ________________ *(play)* golf is not a real sport, which is definitely not true.
3. I admit ________________ *(eat)* the last piece of apple pie, Mum. Sorry, but it just tasted so good.
4. I will never forget your ________________ *(lie)* to me so cruelly last month. How could you be so mean?
5. I can't tolerate you ________________ *(be)* late again.
6. I'm really proud of myself! I finally finished ________________ *(redecorate)* my room, all by myself!
7. Mum really didn't mind us ________________ *(come)* home late yesterday. I had texted her before and she was fine with it.
8. Steve doesn't resent you always ________________ *(forget)* his birthday. He is very easy on that.
9. I, on the other hand, really appreciate you ________________ *(remember)* my last birthday.
10. Most people enjoy ________________ *(hug)* by their friends.
11. Jennifer forgot ________________ *(tell)* by her teacher to wait outside the teacher's room. That's why she is in big trouble now.
12. Studies show that ________________ *(serve)* quickly is very important for costumers in restaurants.
13. For me, ________________ *(cheat)* on is a no-go in a relationship.
14. I truly hate ________________ *(photograph)* when I eat.

37 ! Complete the sentences with a fitting verb from D.

EXAMPLE Why do you *deny* having taken my car? I saw you leaving in it.

1. Hmmm. This strawberry cheesecake is fantastic. I can't .... having a second piece.
2. Yesterday, Paolo simply .... chatting up that cute girl he'd met at the bar. And she really fell for him!
3. Don't panic, Monica. I absolutely don't .... you dating my ex-boyfriend. I'm over him.
4. It's such a pity you didn't .... cheating in the last English test. Mr Miller would have shown some pity if you had.
5. Last year, Joe definitely .... being expelled from school for behaving indecently at the school prom.
6. Don't give up! .... practising and you will succeed.
7. I really .... your offering me a place to stay for the night. Thank you so much.
8. Sheldon .... people offering to shake his hand. He fears catching a cold or some illness from other people.
9. I think Bertha .... having a coke. Can you get one for her?
10. What shall we do now? I .... going to the movies – the new James Bond is on at the Odeon.
11. Losing weight .... doing a lot of sports, apart from eating less.
12. We fully .... you leaving the team. Having a baby is time consuming and you must sort out your priorities.
13. My parents would never .... me having a boyfriend! They even freak out when I want to go out with one of my best friends.

38 !! Translate the sentences using verbs from D.

EXAMPLE Die Erwachsenen gingen weiter, obwohl die Kinder müde waren.
The grown-ups kept going although the kids were tired.

1. Sie gab zu, dass sie Unrecht gehabt hatte.

2. Ich vermisste es, geliebt zu werden.

3. Alberto empfahl, den Bus zu nehmen.

4. Sue zögerte es hinaus, Zack zu sagen, dass sie Schluss machen wollte.

5. Meine Katze genoss es, von meinen Freunden gestreichelt zu werden.

6. Cathy bestritt, den Aufsatz aus dem Internet heruntergeladen zu haben.

7. Ich würde jetzt wirklich gerne spazieren gehen.

8. Johnny vermisste es, Mia lachen zu hören.

9. Es macht uns wirklich nichts aus, wenn du früher gehst.

10. Das rechtfertigt es nicht, mich anzulügen.

11. Angie wird mir nie verzeihen, dass ich ihre beste Freundin geküsst habe.

E Wenn ein Verb auf eine Präposition folgt → GERUND

E1 preposition + gerund

Can you eat an apple ***without using*** *your hands?*
They saved the man's life ***by giving*** *him a blood transfusion.*
Jackie says a prayer ***before going*** *to bed.*

E2 ! verb + preposition + gerund (phrasal verbs)

Please let me ***apologise for being*** *so rude on the phone yesterday.*
Many young girls ***dream of becoming*** *famous models.*
My parents often ***talk about buying*** *a bigger house.*

accuse of	beschuldigen	*count on*	zählen auf	*rely on*	sich verlassen auf
adjust to	anpassen an	*decide against*	entscheiden gegen		
agree with	zustimmen	*depend on*	abhängen von	*save from*	bewahren vor
aim at	abzielen auf	*delight in*	erfreuen an	*see about*	kümmern um
apologise for	entschuldigen	*despair of*	verzweifeln	*speak about*	sprechen über
approve of	dafür sein	*devote to*	widmen		
ask about	erkundigen	*die of*	sterben an	*speak of*	sprechen von
begin by	beginnen mit	*disapprove of*	dagegen sein	*specialise in*	spezialisieren
believe in	glauben an	*dream of*	träumen von	*spend on*	ausgeben für
benefit from	profitieren von	*escape from*	entkommen	*stop from*	abhalten von
blame for	tadeln für	*forget about*	vergessen	*succeed in*	Erfolg haben
boast of	prahlen mit	*forgive for*	verzeihen	*suspect of*	verdächtigen
brag about	angeben mit	*give up*	aufhören	*take part in*	teilnehmen an
care for	kümmern um	*go on*	weitermachen	*talk about*	sprechen über
carry on	weitermachen	*insist on*	bestehen auf		
charge with	vorwerfen	*look forward to*	sich freuen auf	*talk into*	überreden zu
complain of	klagen über	*look into*	näher ansehen	*thank for*	danken für
concentrate on	sich konzentrieren auf	*object to*	protestieren, dagegen sein	*think about*	nachdenken über
confess to	gestehen	*prevent from*	hindern an	*think of*	denken an
consist of	bestehen aus	*put off*	aufschieben	*vote against*	dagegen stimmen
cope with	fertig werden mit	*refrain from*	unterlassen		

E3 ! noun + preposition + gerund

What's the ***advantage of speaking*** *foreign languages?*
Travelling is a great ***way of meeting*** *new people and* ***(of) learning*** *about their ways of life.*
There's really ***no point (in) asking*** *him for help again. He won't do it!*

advantage of	Vorteil von	*danger of*	Gefahr	*point of*	Zweck, Sinn
alternative to	Alternative zu	*doubt about*	Zweifel an	*no point (in)*	keinen Sinn
art of	Kunst zu	*gift of*	Begabung für	*reason for*	Grund für
aversion to	Abneigung gegen	*experience in/ with*	Erfahrung in/ bei	*interest in*	Interesse an
chance of	Gelegenheit zu	*idea of*	Idee, Gedanke	*way of*	Art und Weise
choice between	Wahl zwischen	*opportunity of*	Gelegenheit zu	*freedom of*	(Wahl-)Freiheit

39 ! Find the correct preposition to the verbs.

EXAMPLE Thank you for saving me *from* making the biggest mistake of my life.

1. If I were you, I wouldn't brag .... dating three girls at the same time.
2. Why couldn't you prevent your dog .... eating my steak?
3. Forget .... asking Pia for a date. She's with Jim.
4. If you want to write a good essay, you must begin .... collecting information and ideas.
5. Don't try to talk me .... accepting your offer. I won't.
6. Mother Teresa devoted most of her life .... saving children.
7. I simply must rely .... you telling me the truth.
8. Please, don't insist .... dyeing your hair green. I would hate it.
9. I am so looking forward .... seeing David Guetta live.
10. Please, just confess .... having forgotten to hand in the book.
11. Why do some people not even refrain .... smoking when there is a no-smoking sign?
12. Last Sunday I finally succeeded .... finishing my book.
13. You can't blame me .... missing the train.

40 ! Find the correct preposition to the nouns.

EXAMPLE What's the advantage *of* buying a prepaid mobile phone?

1. Ms Bowler has got a lot of experience .... teaching teenagers.
2. We would love to learn the art .... painting by Bob Ross.
3. What's the point .... waiting for them? Let's just go.
4. I can understand your aversion .... singing in front of people.
5. He has no doubts .... her being faithful.
6. What's the alternative .... writing an email? Making a call?
7. There is no point .... trying to convince her. She won't give in.

41 !! Complete the sentences with a verb from E2 and the verbs in brackets.

EXAMPLE Last year, I *was blamed for bullying / was accused of bullying* (*vorwerfen – bully*) one of my classmates. In fact, it was he who bullied me.

1. Sometimes, you must simply ______ (*zählen auf – support*) by your friends.
2. It must be hard for doctors to ______ (*fertig werden mit – tell*) patients that they will die.
3. I wouldn't ______ (*dagegen sein – have*) another drink.
4. Don't ______ (*aufschieben – write*) the letter of application. You are perfect for that job.
5. Please ______ (*stimmen gegen – test*) cosmetics on animals. It's not ethical!
6. Cats do not easily ______ (*anpassen an – live*) in new surroundings.
7. Finally I can ______ (*profitieren von – work*) so hard.

42 ! Complete the sentences with a noun from E3 and the verbs in brackets.

EXAMPLE It's hard to have the *choice between sleeping and partying.* (*Wahl zwischen – schlafen – feiern*).

1. It seems like you really have the ______ (*Geschenk – zufrieden zu sein*) with what you have.
2. You must seize the ______ (*Gelegenheit – reisen*) all over the world by accepting that job offer.
3. What is the ______? (*Grund dafür, dass du zu spät bist*)

43 !! Translate the sentences. Use gerund forms.

EXAMPLE Warum bestehst du darauf, diese Krawatte zu tragen?
Why are you insisting on wearing that tie?

1. Ich denke darüber nach, meinen Job zu kündigen.

2. Mike freut sich darauf, seine Freunde zu treffen.

3. Rechne nicht damit, in die Disco gelassen zu werden.

4. Meiner Katze Mia missfällt es, wenn ich auf ihrem Platz liege.

5. Gib mir nicht die Schuld dafür, dass wir spät dran sind.

6. Nino entschuldigte sich, dass er meinen Geburtstag vergessen hatte.

7. Vergiss es, auf diese Party zu gehen!

8. Bitte rette mich davor, den gleichen Fehler wieder zu machen.

9. Die Regierung entschied sich gegen den Bau neuer Autobahnen.

10. Wir geben nicht genug Geld aus, um den Armen zu helfen.

11. Manche Menschen widmen ihr ganzes Leben der Suche nach Gold.

E4 ! to be + adjective + preposition + gerund

*We **are** all very **excited about going** to New York in summer.*
*Marvin **has** always **been good at finding** clever excuses for himself.*
*Lydia **is worried about meeting** Joe again at the party.*
*I think fewer and fewer people **are interested in reading** books today.*

to be …					
accustomed to	gewöhnt an	*famous for*	berühmt für	*ready for*	bereit für
afraid of	fürchten vor	*far from*	weit entfernt von	*responsible for*	verantwortlich für
alarmed at	sich ängstigen	*fed up with*	leid sein, satt haben	*right about*	Recht haben
angry at/ about	zornig auf	*fined for*	Geldstrafe bekommen	*sad about*	traurig über
annoyed at/ about	verärgert über	*fond of*	gern haben, mögen	*shocked at/ about*	schockiert über
appropriate for	geeignet für	*free from*	frei von	*sick (and tired) of*	es (gründlich) satt haben
astonished at	erstaunt über	*glad at/about*	froh über	*sorry for/ about*	leidtun, bedauern
bad at/in	schlecht bei	*good at*	gut bei	*sure about*	sicher wegen
capable of	fähig	*happy about*	glücklich über	*surprised at*	überrascht von
certain of	sicher	*impressed by/ with*	beeindruckt von	*tired from*	müde von
charged with	angeklagt, beschuldigt	*in charge of*	verantwortlich für	*tired of*	es satt haben, genug haben
clever at	geschickt in	*interested in*	interessiert an	*thankful for*	dankbar für
crazy about	verrückt nach	*involved in*	verstrickt/verwickelt in	*used for*	verwendet für
conscious of	bewusst	*keen on*	begeistert von	*used to*	gewöhnt an
disappointed at	enttäuscht über	*notorious for*	berüchtigt für	*worry about*	sich Sorgen machen über
excited about	aufgeregt über	*pleased with/ about*	erfreut über	*wrong about*	falsch liegen
		proud of	stolz über		

F ! *gerund* nach bestimmten Fügungen *(phrases)*

*A famous song by Andrew Gold is called "**Thank you for being** a friend".*
***What about ordering** some pizzas and coke tonight?*
*I **can't bear listening** to this noise any longer. Let's leave!*

can't bear *can't stand*	nicht ertragen können	*it's no use* *it's little use*	es hat keinen/ wenig Sinn	*to be busy*	eifrig dabei/ beschäftigt sein
can't help	nicht anders können	*waste one's time*	Zeit verschwenden	*to feel like*	zu Mute sein, danach fühlen
it's worth	wert sein	*How/What about …?*	Wie wär's mit …?	*thank you for*	danke für
it's no good	es ist sinnlos	*there's no denying*	es hat keinen Sinn zu leugnen		

44 ! **Open gap fill: Find the correct preposition to the adjectives.**

Hi Tim,

I'm sorry *for* not having answered your last mail any sooner – but I've been quite busy recently. School's been a mess – you were right **1.** .... warning me about year 9 maths. But there is also good news! ☺

Guess what happened yesterday? You know – I've always been impressed **2.** .... fast cars, but I was sure **3.** .... never being able to drive a race car myself. I was wrong! Last Sunday, my dad took me to a race circuit. When I saw the car he had rented for me I felt so excited **4.** .... climbing in that my heart beat twice as fast. Of course, I wasn't allowed to drive it alone – there was a man who was in charge **5.** .... bringing me back safely. When I started the engine I was astonished **6.** .... hearing such a loud noise – but I quickly became accustomed **7.** .... it. Touching the steering wheel made me feel totally keen **8.** .... gripping it tight and hitting the gas. Of course, as I wasn't used **9.** .... handling such a powerful vehicle, I first had to take it slow. But I quickly got the hang of it. I would never have dreamed of being capable **10.** .... steering a race car on my own – but I proved myself wrong. Of course, I was conscious **11.** .... keeping control. Cruising through the bends and powering down the straights, I felt nothing but exhilaration. After twenty minutes, I climbed out of the car, happy – but also a bit dizzy. I felt so proud **12.** .... having driven solo. But then, to my surprise, it got even better: My co-pilot took off his helmet – and I was totally shocked **13.** .... finding out who he was – Jacques Villeneuve! You might probably know him – he was that crazy looking young driver in the nineties who was famous at the time **14.** .... becoming the youngest world champion.

I'm so thankful **15.** .... having been allowed to experience such a great day.

Yours, Max

45 ! **Open gap fill: Complete the text with a suitable phrase from F.**

Julie: Hi Sarah. How are things going?

Sarah: Sorry Julie. I'm in a really bad mood today. You know, I ***can't stand/bear*** the boys at our school anymore.

Julie: Why's that? Tell me what you are talking about.

Sarah: See, there is this guy, Philipp. He's my ex-boyfriend's best friend. Last Saturday, he got a little drunk and told everyone he was in love with me. And now I really ______________ thinking that everyone is staring and laughing at me.

Julie: But Sarah, ______________ worrying about something like this. Kids always need someone to laugh about. If I were you I would just not listen to them. And by the way, Philipp is really cute. ______________ seizing the opportunity and asking him for a date? That might really give them something to talk about.

Sarah: Sorry Julie, but I really don't ______________ giving them even more reason to talk about me. And besides, I ______________ minding my own problems. We got back that English test, and I got an F! My parents are definitely going to kill me.

Julie: Well, it's ______________ seeing only the negative side of everything. I wrote an F too. Most of us did. Mr Fletcher will have to let us resit the test. So, let's not ______________ complaining and nagging. You know what? Come over tomorrow and we'll study for the test together. And by the way, Philipp will be there too.

Sarah: You are hopeless, Julie. But I'll be there. ______________ cheering me up a little bit. And who knows, I might probably give Philipp a chance …

46 !! **Translate the sentences. Use words from E4 and F.**

EXAMPLE Ich bin sehr erfreut darüber, dass ich so einen guten Test geschrieben habe.
I am very pleased with/about having written such a good test.

1. Chris ist sich nicht bewusst, Dora gegenüber untreu gewesen zu sein.

2. Studenten sind dafür berüchtigt, wilde Partys zu feiern.

3. Wir sind es nicht gewohnt, so lange zu warten.

4. Trevor ist sehr geschickt darin, gute Ausreden zu finden.

5. Es lässt sich nicht leugnen, dass das Trinken von Alkohol deinen Körper schädigt.

6. Mir ist nach einem Schläfchen zumute.

7. Ich kann es nicht mehr ertragen, diesen Song zu hören.

8. Armin ist begeistert davon, Schifahren zu gehen.

9. Maria ist verärgert darüber, dass sie ihren Schlüssel verloren hat.

G ! *gerund* nach Verben, die Vorliebe oder Abneigung ausdrücken

like – love – enjoy – dislike – hate

*Do you **like** or **dislike** **dancing**, Britney? – I love it!*
*I **love** downhill **skiing**, but I really **hate** cross-country **skiing**.*
*When I was young, I really **enjoyed** **hiking** in the mountains with Dad.*

Einige Verben kommen sowohl mit dem *gerund* als auch mit dem Infinitiv vor. Nähere Informationen dazu im Kapitel *gerund or infinitive* ab Seite 60.

H ! *gerund* anstelle von Temporalsätzen (Zeitsätzen)

Die **„Verkürzung" von Gliedsätzen** mit Hilfe des *gerunds* ist ein typisches Merkmal der gehobenen englischen Sprache. Sie tritt daher vor allem in der geschriebenen Sprache auf. Die Verkürzung mit Hilfe des *gerund* ist nur dann möglich, wenn Hauptsatz und Gliedsatz dasselbe Subjekt haben. Ob Hauptsatz oder Gliedsatz am Beginn steht, ist dabei unwichtig.

***After Mum had graduated** from college, **she** started working as a teacher.*
***After graduating** from college, **Mum** started working as a teacher.* Oder:

*Mum started working as a teacher **after she had graduated** from college.*
*Mum started working as a teacher **after graduating** from college.*

***When Leon left** the house this morning, **he** noticed a strange smell in the air.*
***On leaving** the house this morning, **Leon** noticed a strange smell in the air.*

*Fiona switched off all the lights **before she lit** the candles on the cake.*
*Fiona switched off all the lights **before lighting** the candles on the cake.*

I ! by + *gerund* anstelle eines „indem-Satzes"

Sätze mit „indem" sind Modalsätze; sie sagen uns, auf welche Art und Weise etwas geschieht.

*The prisoners escaped **by digging** a tunnel under the wall.*
(… indem sie einen Tunnel gruben.)

***By turning** everything upside down, we finally found the missing keys.*
(Indem wir alles auf den Kopf stellten, fanden wir endlich …)

47 ! Combine the sentences by using gerund forms (if possible).

EXAMPLE Zac found out that his girlfriend had had an affair with his best friend. He broke up with her.
After finding out that his girlfriend had had an affair with his best friend, Zac broke up with her. / Zac broke up with his girlfriend after finding out that she had had an affair with his best friend.

1. Samira was getting on the train. She lost her balance and crashed into a good looking boy.

2. Nadia rang Simon's doorbell. Before that she checked herself twice in her mirror.

3. Marshall answered his phone. His father told him that he wanted to visit him the next day.

4. Donna realised that her car was gone. She called the police.

5. Jack came into kitchen. He saw that his mum had already prepared a big breakfast for him.

6. My cat ate the mouse. Before that she played with it for half an hour.

48 ! **Combine the sentences into one. Use by-gerund forms.**

EXAMPLE You can win this TV. You must send in the correct answer to our question.
You can win this TV by sending in the correct answer to our question.
By sending in the correct answer to our question you can win this TV.

1. You can switch between the two screens. You must press this button.

2. Gina accidentally opened a letter addressed to her husband. She found out about the surprise holiday to Dubai he had planned for her.

3. I randomly keyed in numbers into the hotel room safe. This way, I found out how to open it.

4. I taught my dog to sit up and beg. I gave him little treats.

5. We managed to complete painting our house. We invited all our friends over to help us.

6. Julia embarrassed her best friend. She did not tell her that something green was stuck between her teeth.

49 !! Open gap fill: Complete the text with an appropriate expression.

Laser Tag

Do you *fancy* having the greatest time in your life? Have you always been **1.** .... on experiencing something completely different as you are totally **2.** .... with your daily routines? Then join us in a game of Laser Tag.

This is a sport where you score points **3.** .... tagging other players' vests with an infrared targeting device that you hold in your hands. Although this may sound a bit like playing war, you will soon find out that in reality, laser tagging is nothing but fun. The **4.** .... of playing Laser Tag, compared to playing paintball, is that you do not get hurt. As running is forbidden, there is no **5.** .... of accidentally bumping into another player. And even if you are inexperienced at playing computer games, you will soon learn how to **6.** .... with the equipment. Once you have got **7.** .... to spotting and targeting the other players in the dark environment, you will soon improve your score. Sure, there is no **8.** .... that people with experience in this kind of game might be at an advantage at first. But once the playing mode changes, for example to "Zombie mode", more inexperienced players have a real shot at winning the game. There, you must **9.** .... the zombie players from "biting" you so as not to let them turn you into a zombie too. You will be impressed **10.** .... the number of different ways of playing Laser Tag. You may even **11.** .... having your next birthday party at a Laser Tag venue. Your friends might be totally **12.** .... at finding out about this new and fun sport. And **13.** .... overcomimg their initial doubts, your friends will **14.** .... you for having organised such an awesome party.

So, don't **15.** .... your time feeling bored – give tagging a try.

INFINITIVE – INFINITIV, NENNFORM

A Grundsätzliches über den Infinitiv / die Nennform

- Der Infinitiv wird auch Nennform genannt. Er ist die 1. Stammform des Verbs (auf Englisch: 1st *form* oder *base form*).
- Der Infinitiv tritt **mit und ohne to** auf.

B ! Infinitiv nach einem Verb mit to

*I **happened to find** the records my dad had collected as a teen.*
*Rupert doesn't **care to take** part in our activities.*
*Victoria **managed to finish** the puzzle first.*
*The man **pretended not to look** in our direction.*

afford	sich leisten	*expect*	erwarten	*promise*	versprechen
agree	zustimmen	*fail*	scheitern	*refuse*	sich weigern
appear	scheinen	*happen*	(zufällig)	*remind*	jem. erinnern
arrange	regeln	*hesitate*	zögern	*seem*	scheinen
ask	bitten	*hope*	hoffen	*swear*	schwören
attempt	versuchen	*intend*	beabsichtigen	*tend*	dazu neigen
care	mögen	*learn*	(er)lernen	*threaten*	drohen
choose	sich für etwas entscheiden	*manage*	zustande bringen, schaffen	*vow*	schwören
claim	behaupten	*offer*	anbieten	*wait*	warten
decide	beschließen	*plan*	planen	*want*	wollen
demand	fordern	*prepare*	sich bereit machen	*wish*	wünschen
				would like	würde gern
deserve	verdienen	*pretend*	so tun, als ob …	*yearn*	sich sehnen

C ! Infinitiv nach einem Verb ohne to

- mit den ***modal verbs***
  *We **can do** it! – I **must go** now. – It **may rain** later today.*
- mit ***let*** **und** ***make*** in der Bedeutung von **„lassen"**
  *They didn't **let** us **leave** the room for two hours.*
  *You can't **make** me **jump** if I don't want to.*
- mit ***had better (not)*** und ***would rather (not)***
  *You**'d better go** now.* → Du solltest jetzt lieber gehen.
  *I**'d rather not stay** here.* → Ich möchte lieber nicht hierbleiben.

D ! Infinitiv nach einem Fragewort

*I didn't know **what to say**.*
*Does anyone know **where to go**?*
*Flora showed me **how to do** it.*
*There were many people there, but I had forgotten **who to ask**.*
*Has nobody told you **when to come**?*

50 !! **Translate the sentences. Use infinitive forms.**

EXAMPLE Ich kann es mir nicht leisten, mit euch auf das Konzert zu gehen.
I can't afford to go to the concert with you.

1. Wir sehnen uns danach, wieder einmal auf Urlaub zu fahren.

....

2. Phil zögerte, das Angebot anzunehmen.

....

3. Samira schaffte es, Ruhe zu bewahren.

....

4. Unsere Katze weigert sich, ohne uns zu essen.

....

5. Du solltest jetzt lieber deinen Test abgeben.

....

6. Wir würden lieber nicht so spät zurückkommen.

....

7. Die Katze zögerte, die neue Katzenklappe zu benutzen.

....

51 ! **Complete the sentences with a suitable infinitive form after a question word.**

EXAMPLE Does anyone know *when* to leave? – Yes! We're leaving at eight.

1. I'm sorry, I didn't know exactly *when* .... I thought the party started at nine.
2. I had no idea *how* .... the meat, but it tasted nice anyway.
3. I had forgotten to take my shopping list with me so I had no clue *what* ....

E ! Infinitiv nach bestimmten Wortarten

Ordnungszahlwörter *the first, the last …*	**Superlative** *the best, the worst …*	***next – only …*** der nächste / der einzige
*The captain is **the last to leave** the ship.*	***The worst** thing **to do** is to stop now.*	*You're the **next to get** in trouble.*
*Columbus was not **the first to reach** America.*	*This cheese was **the cheapest to get**.*	*The **only** thing **to do** now is to run.*

F ! Infinitiv nach einem Adjektiv

*Ladies and gentlemen, I'm very **happy to be** here with you!*
*We're **sorry to announce** that all trains will be late today.*
*It is more and more **important to speak** foreign languages.*
*Was it really **necessary to spend** so much money on sweets?*
*Theo was **too tired to finish** the game.*

G ! Infinitiv nach bestimmten Nomen

*We have no **desire to go** out in this kind of weather.*
*The pilot was asking for **permission to land** immediately.*
*Who gave the **command to pull** back?*
*There is a **tendency not to believe** the news programmes.*

ability	Fähigkeit	*need*	Bedürfnis	*refusal*	Ablehnung
chance	Gelegenheit	*offer*	Angebot	*request*	Bitte
command	Befehl	*opportunity*	Gelegenheit	*right*	Recht
courage	Mut	*permission*	Erlaubnis	*tendency*	Tendenz
decision	Entscheidung	*plan*	Plan	*time*	Zeit
desire	Wunsch, Verlangen	*possibility*	Möglichkeit	*urge*	Drang, Verlangen
failure	Versagen	*promise*	Versprechen	*way*	Art, Weise
freedom	Freiheit	*readiness*	Bereitschaft	*wish*	Wunsch
inclination	Neigung	*reason*	Grund		

H !! *verb + object + infinitive*

	verb	*object*	*infinitive*		
▸ **wie auf Deutsch**					
Michael	***allowed***	***me***	***to drive***	*his car.*	▸ mit to
Nobody	***helped***	***us***	***to put***	*up the tent.*	
Michael	***lets***	***me***	***drive***	*his car.*	▸ ohne to
I'll	***make***	***you***	***feel***	*sorry for this!*	
▸ **anstelle eines dass-Satzes**					
She	***wants***	***me***	***to tell***	*her about you.*	
I don't	***expect***	***you***	***to get***	*an "A" again.*	
Sie	möchte,	dass ich ihr von dir erzähle.			
Ich	erwarte nicht,	dass du wieder ein „Sehr gut" bekommst.			

52 ! Rewrite the sentence. Use infinitive forms with the words in *italics*.

EXAMPLE The best thing *we can do* is to call an ambulance.
The best thing to do is to call an ambulance.

1. The shortest way *you can take* leads through the valley.

   ....

2. This is the best place *for crossing* the river.

   ....

3. Julia, you are the next *who climbs up* the rope.

   ....

4. The only film *we can watch* this summer is the new James Bond.

   ....

53 ! Complete the sentences with a suitable word from G.

EXAMPLE The last time I went to the theatre with my class I felt a sudden ***need/urge*** to sneeze. I couldn't hold it back, so everyone stared at me.

1. Julian, this is just a spider. There is absolutely no .... to jump around and squeal like this!
2. "Mr Jimbal, do we have your .... to leave the classroom?" – "Sure, you may go now."
3. Have you ever had the .... to ride an e-bike? I tried it last week. It was really cool.
4. "Hey Marla! Try this Segway here. It's so much fun." – "Sorry Paolo, I don't think I have the .... to do it. I'm afraid of breaking my leg or something else."
5. Mathew, you have every .... to be angry. I would feel angry too if someone had stolen my bike.

GERUND OR INFINITIVE

A ! Mit gleicher oder ähnlicher Bedeutung

gleiche Bedeutung	ähnliche Bedeutung
begin – start – continue	***verb + infinitive***
*They **continued to play** after a while.* = *They **continued playing** after a while.*	eher bei allgemein gehaltenen Aussagen; nicht bei einzelnen Handlungen *I never see you **do** your homework.*
(dis)like – love – prefer – hate	***verb + ing-form***
*Nick **prefers to walk** to school.* = *Nick **prefers walking** to school.*	eher bei bestimmten, beobachtbaren einzelnen Handlungen *I can see you **doing** your homework!*
In allgemeinen Situationen wird das Gerund jedoch vorgezogen.	

B !! Mit (großem) Unterschied in der Bedeutung

verb + infinitive		*verb + ing-form*
vergessen (werden)	***forget***	vergessen (haben)
*I totally **forgot to call** Julia last night.*		*I'll never **forget meeting** you, Max!*
► notwendige Handlung; darf man nicht vergessen / hätte man nicht vergessen dürfen		► Erinnerung an schon Geschehenes; wird man / sollte man nie vergessen
müssen	***need***	brauchen
*You **need to see** a doctor soon!*		*This fence **needs repairing**.*
► Notwendigkeit, Zwang (aktiv) jemand muss/soll etwas tun		► Notwendigkeit, Zwang (passiv) etwas muss (damit) geschehen
bedauern	***regret***	bedauern
*I will always **regret to tell** you this.*		*I will always **regret telling** you this.*
► Man bedauert etwas, das noch nicht passiert ist, aber gleich passieren wird.		► Man bedauert etwas, das schon passiert ist.
daran denken	***remember***	sich erinnern
*I hope I'll **remember to charge** my mobile phone tonight.*		*Do you **remember talking** to Julia at the party?*
► etwas, das noch nicht passiert ist und woran man auf jeden Fall denken muss/soll		► sich an etwas erinnern, das schon geschehen ist
unterbrechen, um zu …	***stop***	aufhören, beenden
*We **stopped to admire** the view.*		***Stop staring** at the people!*
► eine Tätigkeit unterbrechen, um etwas anderes zu tun; „um zu“		► eine Tätigkeit beenden; mit etwas aufhören
versuchen	***try***	versuchen
*I **tried to catch** the ball, but I couldn't.*		***Try catching** the ball with both hands!*
► schon versucht		► Tipp, wie es besser gehen könnte.

54 !! Gerund or infinitive? Circle the correct version.

EXAMPLE I absolutely hate *going/to go* to weddings.

1. I would really love *dancing/to dance* this tango with you.
2. When we were children, we always watched the squirrels in our garden *chase/chasing* each other.
3. What's that noise over there? Jennifer and Brandon, I can hear you *whisper/whispering*. Please be quiet and listen to what I am saying.
4. Don't forget *to call/calling* your mum. She wants to know that we have arrived safely at our hotel.
5. We'll never forget *watching/to watch* that great sunset on our honeymoon on Hawaii.
6. This hotel room needs *to clean/cleaning*.
7. We really need *to ask/asking* for directions. I have absolutely no clue which way leads to the exit.
8. Look at Sophie! She has been flirting with your boyfriend all evening. Now, do you regret *inviting/to invite* her to your party?
9. I might probably regret *asking/to ask* you this, but are you pregnant?
10. I have no clue why Snowball is meowing like crazy. I remember *to feed/feeding* her in the morning, so she can't be hungry.
11. Please remember *putting/to put* your clothes out in the garden when you return from the party. I don't want the whole house to smell like an ashtray.
12. Stop *to sing/singing* that horrible song! I've just got it out of my head and now it's back. Shame on you.
13. Dad? Can we stop *to go/going* to the restroom? I really need to pee.
14. I tried *calling/to call* you several times, but you didn't answer.
15. Don't try *repairing/to repair* that bike on your own. You know you're hopeless with tools.

55 ! **Gerund or infinitive? Complete the sentences with the correct form of the verbs in brackets.**

1. Sue: I have finally decided **to get** *(get)* a cat.
   Pat: But Sue, why did you decide against ______ *(buy)* a dog? I thought you always wanted to get one.
2. Have you heard about Tim? He stopped ______ *(smoke)* again last week. I wonder how long he will manage ______ *(stay)* off cigarettes this time.
3. Last year, I planned ______ *(redecorate)* my room, but Mum advised me against ______ *(do)* it all by myself.
4. I hate it when my boyfriend pretends ______ *(be)* a complete jerk when his friends are around.
5. I don't deny ______ *(eat)* too much, so you need not remind me ______ *(eat)* less.
6. I miss ______ *(talk)* to you, but you seem ______ *(be)* happy without me.
7. Some of my teachers really tend ______ *(exaggerate)* when they keep telling me that I risk ______ *(fail)* this year.
8. My dog is not used to ______ *(stay)* at home alone. So, when he was small I used ______ *(take)* him to my parents, and now he comes with me to work.
9. Although Gerard swore ______ *(be)* faithful, I clearly remember ______ *(see)* him kissing a girl in the park. So I have vowed ______ *(revenge)* myself.
10. Philipp offered ______ *(take)* me on a sailing trip, but I'm not sure if I should accept.
11. Do you intend ______ *(drink)* that?
12. Don't hesitate ______ *(call)* me.

56 ! Complete the list of verbs that require the infinitive with those from task 55.

agree	aim	appear	arrange
ask	attempt	be able	beg
begin	care	choose	condescend
consent	continue	dare	decide
deserve	detest	expect	fail
forget	get	happen	have
	hope	hurry	
leap	leave	long	
neglect		ought	
prepare		promise	propose
refuse		say	
strive			try
use		wait	want
wish		yearn	

57 !! Translate the sentences. Mind gerund or infinitive forms.

EXAMPLE Dad blieb stehen, um die alte Dame die Straße überqueren zu lassen.
Dad stopped to let the old lady cross the street.

1. Tina darf nicht vergessen, ihrer Oma zum Geburtstag zu gratulieren.

2. Versuche weniger Backpulver für den Kuchen zu verwenden.

3. Der Hund muss gefüttert werden. (mit *need*)

58 !! Open gap fill: High Rope Courses

You are going to read a text about climbing in high rope parks. Some words are missing from the text. Find the correct word for each gap (1–11) and write your answers in the spaces provided at the end of the text. The first one (0) has been done for you.

High Rope Courses

Are you keen **(0)** ____ experiencing the thrill of standing ten metres above the ground, surrounded by rustling leaves and swinging branches? Are you fed up **(1)** ____ being dominated by your fears, and would you like to face them in order to overcome them? If your answer to these questions is a clear YES, you may have found the right place to go: a high rope course.

When you go to a high rope course, you have to begin **(2)** ____ putting on the mandatory gear: the helmet and the harness with the karabiners and the flying fox device. An introductory course helps you to get adjusted **(3)** ____ using your equipment safely. Always remember this golden rule: both karabiners must always and in any case be attached to the safety ropes. Only then will you be safe **(4)** ____ falling ten metres to death or severe injuries.

Once you have learned and proved how to deal **(5)** ____ your equipment, you will be allowed to move onto to the climbing course. You will be astonished **(6)** ____ how quickly you feel familiar **(7)** ____ moving metres above the ground on thin ropes, swinging beams and wobbly nets. Even if you are not used **(8)** ____ rock climbing or bouldering you will enjoy this new experience: for it is not strength that counts, but endurance and courage.

But what is that flying fox device you have read about used **(9)** ____ ? The answer is easy: flying, of course. Once confronted **(10)** ____ a green steel rope you must adjust this special device, sit down in your harness and there you go! Gliding down the rope, you feel as if you were flying. So, are you looking forward **(11)** ____ experiencing this adventure? If yes, then check out where to find the nearest high rope park.

0. on

1. ____________

2. ____________

3. ____________

4. ____________

5. ____________

6. ____________

7. ____________

8. ____________

9. ____________

10. ____________

11. ____________

59 !! Multiple choice: Whale Watching

You are going to read a text about whale watching. Some words are missing from the text. Choose the correct answer (A, B, C or D) for each gap (1–11). Then write your answers in the space provided. The first one (0) has been done for you.

Whale Watching

The sun is glistening off the soft waves of the Pacific Ocean. Seagulls are crying while a heavily loaded boat is taking its passengers out on the windy sea. Why? Because they are looking forward **(0)** ____ whales in their natural surroundings.

You will perhaps be **(1)** ____ finding out that observing whales does not require a four-day boat trip in Alaska. No – if you want to be part of it, you just have to spare four hours for one of those tourists' trips in Monterey, California, or in Provincetown, Massachusetts. Don't be afraid **(2)** ____ on a boat that is packed with other tourists – this time you are not in danger **(3)** ____ ripped off. Of course, your chances **(4)** ____ whales might vary. There are days when you will find yourself surrounded by humpback, killer, blue or minke whales – and you may feel you could really get used **(5)** ____ them. And then there are days when whales might be reluctant **(6)** ____ themselves. But even if you can only watch them from a distance you will be impressed **(7)** ____ them in their natural environment.

So what exactly happens on such a trip? Once you have boarded the boat, the guide starts **(8)** ____ you background information on the whales as well as their natural habitat while the boat takes you closer to the giant mammals. After about an hour you will be able **(9)** ____ seagulls gathering over foamy water. This means that you have reached one of the spots where whales are blowing. The boat will soon circle that spot – and if you wait patiently enough, your patience will be rewarded with the appearance of a majestic tail fin. It may even happen that one of the whales feels tempted to swim alongside your boat, or even jump high in the air. Never stop **(10)** ____ and always hold your camera close at hand – whale activity might happen at any time and place around you.

So, if you see a sign offering whale watching tours, don't hesitate **(11)** ____ this offer. It will be an experience you will never forget.

0	A	to see	B	to check	C	*to seeing*	D	checking
1	A	fascinated in	B	surprised at	C	astonished with	D	interested for
2	A	to climb	B	to drive	C	to climbing	D	of climbing
3	A	to be	B	for being	C	of being	D	to get
4	A	of seeing	B	to see	C	for seeing	D	in seeing
5	A	to observing	B	to observe	C	in observing	D	observing
6	A	at showing	B	of showing	C	showing	D	to show
7	A	to observe	B	at observing	C	by observing	D	observing
8	A	giving	B	for giving	C	from giving	D	on giving
9	A	observing	B	for observing	C	in observing	D	to observe
10	A	to watch	B	watching	C	to watching	D	for watching
11	A	in accepting	B	accepting	C	to accept	D	to accepting

0	1	2	3	4	5	6	7	8	9	10	11
C											

60 !! Word formation: Blobbing

You are going to read a text about the new trend sport, blobbing. Some words are missing from the text. Use the words in brackets to complete each gap (1–10) in the text. Write your answers in the spaces provided at the end of the text. The first one (0) has been done for you.

Blobbing

This summer, a new trend is hitting our lakes: Blobbing. When you pack your towel and your swimwear – do you prefer **(0)** ____ **(get)** active or do you want to lie lazily in the sun? If you would rather go for the first choice, then we might have something for you. Interested? Then read on.

A blob is a partly filled rubber airbag that floats on water. If you decide on **(1)** ____ **(join)** the blobbing competition, you will be asked to either **(2)** ____ **(seat)** on the edge of the blob or jump on the other side. The person sitting will then be catapulted high up in the air, fly over the lake and hit it at random. Some of you may now find it hard to resist **(3)** ____ **(trial)** this cool activity. But be careful – only people older than 12 are permitted **(4)** ____ **(participation)**. The reason is obvious. As you cannot plan how you fly and where you **(5)** ____ **(landing)**, you may fall hard on your head or back. One safety measure is **(6)** ____ **(put)** on a helmet and a neoprene suit. Once you have understood the safety instructions, you can begin **(7)** ____ **(enjoyment)** the fun.

Notice – blobbing is not only a popular hobby, but also a highly competitive sport. In 2012, the first Blobbing Battle took place in Austria, with people beginning to **(8)** ____ **(competition)** against each other. Now, many participants are devoted to **(9)** ____ **(practise)** this sport. So, if you are looking forward to **(10)** ____ **(prove)** your blobbing skills, check out where the next competition is going to take place and be part of it.

0. *getting/to get*

1. ____________

2. ____________

3. ____________

4. ____________

5. ____________

6. ____________

7. ____________

8. ____________

9. ____________

10. ____________

61 !! Banked gap fill: Dog Geocaching

You are going to read a text about a new hobby that keeps dogs and owners fit. Some words are missing from the text. Choose from the list (A–P) the correct word for each gap (1–12) in the text. There are three extra words that you should not use. Write your answers in the space provided. The first one (0) has been done for you.

Dog Geocaching

Have you ever thought of **(0)** ...... something completely new? Are you fed up **(1)** ...... your dog on the same old boring walks every day? Does your dog object **(2)** ...... the same unchallenging things week after week? We have got the solution: dog geocaching.

The aim of this sport is finding a cache, a kind of "treasure", hidden in a forest. You and your dog are supposed **(3)** ...... the cache – with the help of a GPS unit and your dog's nose. As a team you have to trace one clue after the other, which are all carefully hidden in the forest and will finally lead you to the treasure.

But how do you find the clues? First, you must start **(4)** ...... your dog to smell the clues, which all have the same fragrance. Let's assume it's vanilla soap. You hold the soap in front of your dog's nose. When your dog moves towards the soap, you reward it with a treat. Now place the soap a bit farther away from your companion, rewarding it again with a treat when it remembers **(5)** ...... its smell. Gradually, you train your dog until it manages to find the soap in the hidden place.

Now that your dog has learned to identify the clues with its nose, it is ready to be taken on the caching tour. Your GPS unit will lead you and your dog towards the first clue, but you will find out that it fully depends on your dog's **(6)** ...... skills. You will see that your pet just can't help **(7)** ...... to the hidden clue once unleashed. The more clues you and your companion find, the closer you will feel as a team.

So, what can you expect at the end of the tour? The treasure, of course. This features snacks and treats for your dog, as well as for you. After running through the woods for about two hours all four-legged and two-legged participants will most certainly enjoy **(8)** ...... in the shade of the trees, eating and drinking their rewards.

And if you are not yet convinced **(9)** ...... your dog on a geocaching tour, just read some of the comments of people who have already done it. Lisa: "I absolutely enjoyed **(10)** ...... Cindy on the tour. I've finally found a hobby which we both love." Jack: "Geocaching with my dog Frodo has turned out to be the best thing ever. I'd love **(11)** ...... that with Frodo again; let's see what the future holds". Monica: "I absolutely do not regret **(12)** ...... in a geocaching tour with Bacon. We had the most exciting time together. I never knew I had a true tracking dog at home."

So, what about you? Grab your partner and give it a try.

A	to do	**B**	to doing	**C**	to find	**D**	to follow
E	following	**F**	to learn	**G**	participating	**H**	relaxing
I	running	**J**	smelling	**K**	taking	**L**	by taking
M	of taking	**N**	with taking	**O**	training	**P**	*trying*

0	1	2	3	4	5	6	7	8	9	10	11	12
P												

LINKING WORDS – SATZVERKNÜPFER

A Grundsätzliches über Satzverknüpfer

Satzverknüpfer ermöglichen die **inhaltliche und sprachliche Verbindung** von Wörtern, Wortgruppen und Sätzen. Erst sie erlauben uns, **verschiedenartige Zusammenhänge** wie die folgenden einfach und verständlich auszudrücken.

B *addition* – Hinzufügen

and	und
both ... and	sowohl ... als auch
not only ... but also	nicht nur ... sondern auch
also, besides	ebenfalls, auch, außerdem
in addition (to)	außerdem, überdies
furthermore, moreover	außerdem, überdies, darüber hinaus

C *alternative* – Wahlmöglichkeit

or	oder
either ... or	entweder ... oder
neither ... nor	weder ... noch
rather than	eher/lieber ... als, (A) und nicht (B)
otherwise, or else	sonst, ansonsten, andernfalls

D *cause and effect, reason* – Ursache und Wirkung, Grund

therefore, (and) so	daher, deshalb, also
so that	damit, sodass
so ... that	so ... dass
for (nie am Satzanfang!)	denn, weil, da
as, because, since	da, weil
in order to / so as to	um ... zu, so ... dass
because of, on account of (mit Nomen)	wegen
due to, owing to (mit Nomen)	aufgrund, infolge, wegen
if only	wenn auch (nur)
therefore, (and) so	daher, deshalb, also
hence	daher, deshalb, infolgedessen
as a consequence/result	daher, infolgedessen, somit
consequently	folglich, somit, dementsprechend
thus	folglich, so
accordingly	folglich, dementsprechend, demgemäß

ACHTUNG!

Stehen die meisten dieser Satzverknüpfer am Satzanfang, musst du ein Komma setzen!

62 ! Addition – Rewrite the sentence using words from B.

EXAMPLE *The apple pie was fresh. It was also delicious.*
The apple pie was fresh and delicious.

63 ! Alternative – Rewrite the sentences using words from C.

EXAMPLE I don't like wine. I don't like beer.
I like neither wine nor beer.

1. Would you like wine? Would you like beer?

2. Tim would have bought the flat if it hadn't been sold.

   The flat had been sold.

64 ! Cause and effect, reason – Fill in the correct forms from D.

EXAMPLE Paul felt tired. ***Therefore***, he went to bed early.

1. We'll look after your pet ________ you can enjoy your holiday.
2. The ice cream tasted ________ awesome ________ I had a second one.
3. He left the party ________ he had no reason to stay.
4. Tim studied for three weeks ________ pass the history test.
5. Thousands of people died ________ a disastrous earthquake.
6. I would feel so much better ________ it stopped raining.
7. Mia finally passed the test. ________ she felt very happy.
8. Millions of fish had died, so prices increased ________.

E comparison – Vergleich

(not) as … as	(nicht) so … wie
more/less/fewer … than	mehr/weniger … als
as if, as though	als ob, als wenn
similarly, likewise	ebenso, gleichermaßen
in contrast (to)	im Gegensatz (zu), dagegen
unlike	im Gegensatz zu, zum Unterschied von, anders als

F condition – Bedingung

if/whether	ob
unless	wenn nicht; außer; ausgenommen, dass
only if	nur (dann), wenn
even if	auch wenn, selbst wenn
whether (…) or not	ob … oder nicht
or else, otherwise	andernfalls, sonst
provided (that)	vorausgesetzt, dass
in case, in the event (that)	falls; für den Fall, dass

G contrast – Gegensatz

but – but still	aber – aber trotzdem/dennoch
yet	doch, dennoch
though, although, even though	obwohl
whereas, while	während, wohingegen
despite, in spite of	trotz
regardless of	ungeachtet, ohne Rücksicht auf
however	jedoch
nevertheless, nonetheless, still	dennoch, trotzdem
on the other hand	andererseits, hingegen
on the contrary	im Gegensatz, im Gegenteil, vielmehr
in contrast (to)	im Gegensatz (zu), dagegen
unlike	im Gegensatz zu, zum Unterschied von

H emphasis – Nachdruck

undoubtedly, clearly	zweifellos, zweifelsohne, ohne Frage
obviously	offensichtlich, offenbar
in fact	genau genommen, eigentlich, tatsächlich
especially, particularly	besonders, insbesondere, ausdrücklich
In general (Satzanfang), ***generally***	allgemein, im Allgemeinen, überhaupt
above all	vor allem, vor allen Dingen, erst recht
admittedly	zwar, allerdings, zugegebenermaßen
naturally, of course	natürlich, gewiss, selbstverständlich

65 ! Comparison – Use every word from E.

EXAMPLE My car goes 180 mph. Yours, too. So, my car is *as fast as* your car. *(fast)*

1. My cat weighs 8 pounds, my dog 20. Obviously, a cat is ………… as a dog. *(heavy)*
2. Jim has got one brother and Mary has got three. So Mary has got ………… brothers than Jim.
3. According to the Forbes' list 2013, Carlos Slim Helu owns 73 billion dollars and Bill Gates 67 billion dollars. So, Mr Gates owns ………… money than Mr Helu.
4. We own three cars, our neighbour only two. Thus, our neighbour owns ………… cars than we do.
5. Sometimes, my cat Susi acts ………… she were a dog. Then, she follows me wherever I go. In short, she acts ………… a normal cat.
6. Veronica performed excellently yesterday. Tamara did ………… . *(ebenso)*
7. Jacob speaks English, Greek and Spanish. Maurice speaks only English. ………… Jacob, Maurice speaks only one language.

66 ! Condition – Use every word from F.

1. I don't know *if/whether* Tina will accept your apology, but you won't find out ………… you ask her.
2. ………… you ask Tina for an apology will you know if she accepts it.
3. I would never buy such a horribly expensive car, ………… I had a million dollars.
4. Let me know ………… you buy that car.
5. Feed the dog, ………… it won't stop barking.
6. ………… you've read the book, you'll know the answer.

67 ! Contrast – Use the words from G.

EXAMPLE Christian knows that his girlfriend has cheated on him, **but still/yet** he would never break up.

1. ______ Sue loves cherries, she didn't eat any.
2. Declan sat on the bench ______ everyone warned him that it had been freshly painted.
3. I enjoy swimming, ______ my best friend prefers dancing.
4. ______ winter tourism saw a huge increase in 2013, summer tourism plummeted.
5. ______ his allergy to flowers, Michael offered his girlfriend a huge bouquet when he proposed to her.
6. Michael is allergic to flowers. ______, he offered his girlfriend a huge bouquet when he proposed to her.
7. On the one hand, dogs are good companions. ______, they need a lot of attention. ______ dogs, cats are much more autonomous.
8. ______ most dogs, cats can be left alone for several hours.

68 !! Emphasis: Rewrite the underlined sentences using a matching linking word from H to give emphasis.

EXAMPLE Ben joined our company a long time ago. He came here ten years ago.
In fact, he came here ten years ago.

1. The company's numbers show irregularities. Some money has been stolen.

   ______

2. New communication methods have had a huge impact on working life. People prefer writing emails to making direct phone calls. *(allgemein)*

   ______

3. Serena loves spending her holidays at the sea. She enjoys going to the Côte d'Azur. *(besonders)*

   ______

69 !! Complete the sentences with the correct linking word.

EXAMPLE *Not only* do school trips have to be instructive, they should also be entertaining.

1. ____________ rising oil prices, commuters are organising protests.
2. ____________ the number of smokers is constantly rising, health organisations are increasing their anti-smoking campaigns.
3. Steve and I split up ____________ things between us had changed.
4. Rapid weather changes might be ____________ climate change.
5. ____________ explanation might be that these effects are totally random.
6. I would have invited him ____________ he had asked.
7. I would ask her personally ____________ send her an e-mail.
8. ________________ the fact that this year's spring arrived rather late, many bees are dying of hunger.
9. Many countries are threatening to sell their gold deposits. ____________ the gold price is dropping.
10. The ship crashed into the ice-berg, and ____________ it sank quickly.
11. ____________ many anxious customers withdrew all their money from their bank accounts, some banks went bankrupt.
12. Steve finally realised what he had done to Maya by not asking her to go to the prom with him. ____________ he apologised by offering her a necklace with his name engraved in a little heart.
13. Steve ____________ apologised for forgetting Maya's birthday, but he also offered her a beautiful necklace as a present.
14. Last March, an unexpected snowstorm hit the Irish coast. ____________ ____________, many farmers lost a great proportion of their sheep.
15. You can ____________ send Mia an email ____________ call her directly.

70 !! **Tick the correct sentences. Give explanations why the incorrect ones are wrong and/or correct them.**

EXAMPLE On the one hand, language trips are fun. On the other hand, pupils learn a lot about culture and language of the foreign country.
This is not a contrast but an addition! Correct: In addition, pupils learn a lot …

1. George has been working out for three months now, yet he does not see much progress.

2. Sam has been in love with Mia for years. Although, he has never asked her for a date.

3. Joshua didn't feel good yesterday. Despite, he went to the meeting and did a great job there.

4. Dr Jenkins claims that smoking does not cause cancer, whereas Dr Miller supports that opinion.

5. For Patrick had never tasted sashimi before, he was quite surprised at how much he liked it when he first tasted it.

6. Not only drinks my cat beer, he also eats crisps.

7. Since many experts are convinced that pesticides harm bees, the use of those toxic substances has recently been banned in Austria.

8. However most smokers are aware of the fact that smoking kills, the number of nicotine addicts has dramatically risen in the last years.

71 !! Combine the sentences into one using the correct linking word.

EXAMPLE Patrick didn't clean his room. He didn't look after his sister. *(weder – noch)*
Neither did Patrick clean his room, nor look after his sister. / Patrick neither cleaned his room nor looked after his sister.

1. Josh's mum had forbidden him to leave the house. He met his friends at the movies. *(obwohl)*

2. Mark doesn't know the answer to the question. Mark would not help Tim. *(auch wenn)*

3. Aaron hadn't bought new bulbs. He had to light candles for dinner. *(Da)*

4. We went for a walk. There was rain. *(trotz)*

5. We had a wonderful day sailing on the lake. There was great wind. *(aufgrund)*

6. People investing in gold made a huge profit. People buying oil lost a lot of money. *(während)*

7. Charlie stared at Melissa. It seemed he had never seen her before. *(als ob)*

8. Sandra loves music. Joan doesn't. *(Im Gegensatz zu)*

72 ! Banked gap fill: A School Where No-One Speaks English

You are going to read a text about a very special school in England. Some words are missing from the text. Choose from the list (A–L) the correct word for each gap (1–9) in the text. There are two extra words that you should not use. Write your answers in the space provided. The first one (0) has been done for you.

The British School Where No-One Speaks English as a First Language

Gladstone Primary in Peterborough is a happy school with well-behaved pupils in neat uniforms. **(0)** ______ if you stand in the school playground and listen to the children at break time, you will realise why Gladstone has been in the news lately: not one of its 440 pupils speaks English as a first language!

The school in the heart of Peterborough's migrant community is thought to be the only one where English is a second language for all of the pupils. Some can't **(1)** ______ speak a word of English when they start at the school in this city in the East of England.

Official figures show that 358 of Gladstone's pupils are from the Punjab and speak Urdu at home, 23 speak Drie, the official language of government in Afghanistan, 15 speak Lithuanian, and 11 Latvian, **(2)** ______ 16 smaller language groups including Russian, German and Polish.

The head teacher, Christine Parker, considers her pupils' language background as a valuable asset **(3)** ______ a problem. **(4)** ______ the reports by Ofsted, the government body that inspects schools, confirm her opinion. Gladstone was given the grade "good", the second-highest rating, in every aspect.

So how does Gladstone cope with all its different languages? The lessons are in English, but the school has 18 teaching assistants who can help with translating if needed. **(5)** ______ teachers in classes for younger children comment in English on everything the children do, they pick up vocabulary naturally.

(6) ______ does the school not ban children from speaking their mother tongue, but it also respects different cultures. For example, the uniform is navy blue and white, but can include a salwar kameez (trousers and tunic) and headscarf for Muslim girls. Religious education at the school is not mainly Christian, but aims to help children "develop a respect and understanding of the beliefs and customs of others".

(7) ______ some critics say that schools like Gladstone help to create ghetto communities. Children speak their language and are surrounded by their immigrant culture at home, and if most pupils at the school are also immigrants, they never integrate properly.

The school is aware of this potential problem. **(8)** ______ it has taken steps to make more of their children have contact with British-born children. Gladstone has a partnership with another local school with mainly non-immigrant children. Year-5 pupils visit the school once every two weeks to speak English with children their own age.

Gladstone is the school that has been in the news, but in fact, it is just part of a bigger trend in schools across Britain. **(9)** ______ over one million primary and secondary school pupils spoke English as a second language in 2012, compared with about 800,000 in 2007. In 2012, one in six primary school pupils spoke a language other than English at home. Christine Parker says that on a global scale, being bilingual or even multilingual is not unusual. She says, "Not only is most of the world bilingual, a lot of the world is multilingual. We're the odd ones out."

A	Accordingly,	B	And	C	As	D	But
E	even	F	for	G	However,	H	in addition to
I	in contrast to	J	Not only	K	rather than	L	Thus,

0	1	2	3	4	5	6	7	8	9
D									

73 ! Multiple choice: Smartphone Ban at School?

You are going to read a young girl's essay about her opinion on banning smartphones from school. Some words are missing from the text. Choose the correct answer (A, B, C or D) for each gap (1–10). Then write your answers in the space provided. The first one (0) has been done for you.

They may cause cancer and they may harm personal relationships. **(0)** ______, they may also facilitate teaching as well as studying. Yes, the gadget under discussion is the smartphone. **(1)** ______ many schools are thinking of banning it completely from their premises, I want to show that this step might reach a bit too far. **(2)** ______ excluding this versatile gadget from our lives, teachers should help us to deal with it responsibly.

One argument in favour of allowing students to use their smartphones at school is that they make classroom activities much easier. This is due to the fact that there are thousands of classroom friendly applications for smartphones in existence. Take, for example, second language classes. **(3)** ______ looking up new words in old-fashioned dictionaries is wearisome and time-consuming, dictionary apps on smartphones show you the required word within seconds. **(4)** ______, the pronunciation of words or verb forms can be easily checked on this ingenious gadget as well.

(5) ______, using smartphones is an effective and timesaving aid to students who prepare projects, presentations and papers. We all know this situation – there is this presentation that has to be done for biology, for instance, you know that you have some spare time at school to work on it, **(6)** ______ you simply cannot find an available computer to work on. The way out of this dilemma can be so simple. Just take out your smartphone, key some words into a search engine and there you go. The whole of the World Wide Web unfolds in front of you, helping you to do the research you need for your presentation.

(7) ______, smartphones simply cannot be banned from school because they have become an integral part of our lives. We communicate through them, we plan our days with them, we can **(8)** ______ check our blood sugar or blood pressure. Today, smartphones belong in our lives, just as calculators, planners and newspapers do.

(9) ______ I want to stress that smartphones should not become a part of school life. **(10)** ______ can they be important gadgets in the classroom, but also outside of the classroom during study time. Most importantly, smartphones are a part of everyday life, which we cannot deny. So I ask teachers not to think of banning smartphones, but of finding ways to teach us how to use them effectively and responsibly.

0	A	Anyway	B	So	C	*However*	D	Accordingly
1	A	As	B	Yet	C	For	D	So
2	A	Rather than	B	Instead	C	And	D	How
3	A	When	B	As long as	C	Usually	D	Whereas
4	A	Like	B	Yet	C	Moreover	D	As
5	A	In contrast	B	In addition	C	In favour	D	In instants
6	A	but	B	and	C	so	D	for
7	A	And	B	Consequently	C	However	D	Finally
8	A	obviously	B	though	C	even	D	too
9	A	Finally	B	In conclusion	C	What is more	D	Lastly
10	A	So	B	Not only	C	Consequently	D	Since

0	1	2	3	4	5	6	7	8	9	10
C										

74 !! Open gap fill: Rihanna

You are going to read a short text about the life of Rihanna. Some words are missing from the text. Find the correct word and write it into the spaces provided at the end of the text. The first one (0) has been done for you.

Robin Rihanna Fenty, better known as the singer, actress and designer Rihanna, was born on February 20, 1988, in Saint Michael, Barbados. **(0)** ______ Rihanna was raised in a Barbadian family, she grew up listening to Caribbean reggae music, soaking in the rhythm of the Caribbean. Not only was she influenced by her cultural background, **(1)** ______ also by singer-songwriter Shontelle, who was Rihanna's drill sergeant during her time in a sub-military programme. In fact, singing has always been an important part of Rihanna's life. **(2)** ______ at the age of seven she could sing, and when she was in high school she sang in a musical trio with two of her classmates. However, **(3)** ______ the career of many stars, Rihanna's was not pushed by her family. **(4)** ______ to her father's drug addiction, Rihanna had to learn to face tough situations at a very early age and to work hard for her career. **(5)** ______ it did not come as a surprise to her parents when their ambitious daughter left her home country at the age of 16 to move to Connecticut, USA, with Evan Rogers, a producer.

(6) ______ Rihanna's new life in the United States was completely different from her childhood in Barbados, the talented young woman quickly settled in, and after **(7)** ______ a few months she signed a contract with a New York company, Def Jam Recordings. **(8)** ______ her first and second albums received mixed reviews, stressing the fact that many of her songs were still strongly influenced by pop and often very simple, her third album met with a far more enthusiastic response. **(9)** ______ the title of the album, *Good Girl Gone Bad,* shows, Rihanna deliberately opted for a new direction of her image and her musical style. Peaking the charts at number 1 in various countries **(10)** ______ receiving top reviews, Rihanna's new uptempo dance tracks were a huge commercial success. Her musical career was topped with the honorary title of Ambassador for Culture and Youth in her home country, Barbados. However, Rihanna's professional success was marred by personal problems. Falling victim to domestic violence, Rihanna separated from her on-and-off boyfriend Chris Brown, obtaining a restraining order at court. Her musical career **(11)** ______ is still rocketing. Songs like *Rated R: Remixed, Love the Way You Lie* or *S&M* have claimed number 1 spots all over the world, listing Rihanna among the most successful artists of the world.

0. As
1. ______
2. ______
3. ______
4. ______
5. ______
6. ______
7. ______
8. ______
9. ______
10. ______
11. ______

75 !! Word formation: An Alternative Rock Band

You are going to read a text about a somewhat alternative rock band. Some words are missing. Use the words in brackets to complete each gap (1–10) in the text. Write your answers in the spaces provided at the end of the text. The first one (0) has been done for you.

A Village Transformed by Grannies

For years, Buranova, a shabby little village in the **(0)** .... **(Russia)** countryside, was **(1)** .... **(consideration)** a dying place not worth living in – a place left behind and forgotten after an oil-boom, with hardly any young people remaining. Life was anything but **(2) ..... (attraction)**, with farms going bankrupt, houses collapsing, no running water, no infrastructure, no chances and no **(3)** .... **(possible)**. The few village stores that remained sold mainly vodka, and everybody felt that this vicious circle could and would never be broken.

But things did change, and those **(4)** .... **(responsibility)** for the change were eight local women, grannies in fact, who placed second in the European Song Contest in May 2012, in Baku, the capital of Azerbaijan. The little ladies, the oldest already 86, shuffled their way across the stage, wearing traditional costumes while **(5)** .... **(performance)** their song, "*Party for Everyone*", an easy-listening and easy-going rock song with the English chorus: "*Party for everybody – dance! Come on and dance! Come on and dance! Come on and boom boom!*" Their performance was an immediate **(6)** .... **(unsuccessful)**, not only among the 100 million television viewers, but also on YouTube **(7)** .... **(short)** afterwards.

The women's good fortune has not only changed their personal lives, but also **(8)** .... **(transformation)** life in Buranova on the whole. In **(9)** .... **(appreciate)** of the group's performance, the local government is now planning to build a water pipeline, install street lights and introduce high-speed Internet in the village's only school. On their return to Buranova, people cheered and rejoiced, and almost everybody was crying with joy. Nobody could believe that a thing like that would ever **(10)** .... **(happening)** to their little village which seemed to have been forgotten by God for such a long time.

0. *Russian*

1. ....

2. ....

3. ....

4. ....

5. ....

6. ....

7. ....

8. ....

9. ....

10. ....

MODAL VERBS – HILFSZEITWÖRTER DER AUSSAGEWEISE

A Grundsätzliches zu den *modal verbs*

- *Modal verbs* treten **immer gemeinsam mit einem Hauptzeitwort** (Vollverb) auf (außer bei Kurzantworten und *tag questions*).
  Das Hauptzeitwort erscheint dabei **immer im *infinitive*** (*base form*, Nennform), aber **ohne to**.
- *Modal verbs* bilden Frage und Verneinung ohne *do, does* und *did*.
- *Modal verbs* sehen in allen Personen der Ein- und Mehrzahl gleich aus; es gibt keine Endungen wie zB das *3rd person -s*.
- *Modal verbs* besitzen nicht alle „üblichen" Zeitwortformen. Es fehlen:
  - der **Infinitiv** (Nennform, 1. Stammform)
  - das Mittelwort der Gegenwart/***present participle (ing-form)***
  - die ***past form*** (2. Stammform) – außer *can – could*
  - das Mittelwort der Vergangenheit/***past participle*** (3. Stammform)
  - *Modal verbs* haben daher **Ersatzformen** für die fehlenden Verbformen.

B ! *can – may – must*: Ersatzformen und Verneinung

Zeitstufe	können	dürfen	müssen
present	*can*	*can/may*	*must*
past	*could* *was/were able*	*could* *was/were allowed*	*had to*
future	*will be able*	*will be allowed*	*will have to*
present perfect	*have / has been able*	*have / has been allowed*	*have / has had to*
past perfect	*had been able*	*had been allowed*	*had had to*
cond. present	*would be able*	*would be allowed*	*would have to*
conditional perfect	*would have been able*	*would have been allowed*	*would have had to*

Zeitstufe	nicht können	nicht dürfen	nicht müssen
present	*cannot/can't* *am/is/are not able*	*cannot/can't* *may not* → mild ***must not*** → streng *am/is/are not allowed*	**need not** *do/does not have to*
past	*could not/couldn't* *was/were not able*	*could not/couldn't* *was/were not allowed*	*did not have to*
future	*will not / won't be able*	*will not / won't be allowed*	*will not / won't have to*
present perfect	*have not / has not been able*	*have not / has not been allowed*	*have not / has not had to*

ACHTUNG!

could drückt eine allgemeine Fähigkeit aus: *When I was six, I could read.*
was able wird für spezielle Situationen verwendet: *Yesterday I was able to win the match.*

76 ! Modal verbs: Tick ✔ the correct sentences, cross ✘ the wrong ones.

EXAMPLE Do you can play the drums? ✘

1. Normally, I must wash the dishes at home, but this week, I must not do it. I swapped chores with my brother.
2. Will you be allowed to go to Ellie's party next weekend?
3. Before I was able to leave the office yesterday, I had had to answer 34 mails.
4. Aris doesn't must work longer today, so he can invite his girlfriend for dinner.

77 !! *can – may – must*: Complete the dialogue with a correct modal verb. Mind the tense. If necessary, include the words in brackets.

Rick: Hi, Theo! Imagine, I ***have just had to*** *(just)* stay in school for two extra hours.

Theo: How come? ______________________ help one of the teachers, or were you kept in detention?

Rick: No, nothing like that. I had just left the building and wanted to open the lock of my bike when I ______________________ find the key! And as all the buses had already left, I knew that I ______________________ make it on time to my baseball practice without my bike.

Theo: So what did you do? ______________________ find the key?

Rick: No, unfortunately not. After an hour I decided that I ______________________ get help. So I went to the teachers' room and asked if I ______________________ use our DIY bolt cutter.

Theo: And? ______________________ borrow it?

Rick: Luckily, yes. But it took us quite some time to cut the stupid lock. And of course I ______________________ to make it on time to my baseball practice.

Theo: That's too bad. Let's throw some balls now, okay?

C ! SOLLEN

shall (not)	*should (not) – ought (not) to*
Shall we go now?	*Girls should not go there alone.*
What shall I do with you?	*We ought to offer them our help.*
You shall not lie or use excuses.	*Shouldn't you call the police?*
▼ **Fragen und Verbote (veraltet)**	▼ **Rat, Tipp, Hinweis**
to be (supposed) to	*"Do you want (me) to ... ?"*
You're not supposed to say this!	*Do you want us to stay or go?*
I am to be back by 10 p.m.	*What do you want them to do?*
Is Joe supposed to know about it?	*Where do you want me to wait?*
▼ **Erwartung, Forderung**	▼ **Sollen wir ...?** **Willst du, dass sie/ich/wir ... ?**

D ! LASSEN

let	*They did not let us go home.* *Please let me in! I'm freezing!* *Mike let me ride his new bike.*	**zulassen** **erlauben** **gestatten**
make	*Don't make me hate you!* *You can't make me stay here!* *Joe is funny; he makes me laugh.*	**veranlassen** **zwingen** **dazu bringen**
have + object + 3rd form	*I had my hair cut yesterday.* *Sue has her clothes made in Paris.* *We'll have our photos taken tomorrow.*	**etwas machen lassen** **nicht selbst tun**

E ! Redewendungen und Fügungen, die „lassen" bedeuten

Leave me alone!	→ Lass(t) mich in Ruhe!
I left my heart in San Francisco.	→ Ich habe mein Herz ... verloren.
Leave it to Joe. He'll do it!	→ Überlass(t) das Joe. ...
Leave it be!	→ Lass(t) es sein!
Who's left the windows open?	→ Wer hat die Fenster offen gelassen?
Leave us some water!	→ Lass(t) uns etwas Wasser übrig!
Did you leave the light on?	→ Hast du das Licht brennen lassen?
Lass das!	→ *Stop it! – That's enough!*
Nicht fallen lassen!	→ *Don't drop it!*
Lasst es euch schmecken!	→ *Enjoy!*
Sie ließen einen Arzt kommen.	→ *They sent for a doctor.*
Lass dir Zeit!	→ *Take your time!*
Opa lässt sich einen Bart wachsen.	→ *Grandpa is growing a beard.*

78 ! Complete the sentences with a suitable form for *sollen*.

EXAMPLE *Do you want me* to help you? – Yes, please. That would be great. Take the broom and sweep the terrace, please.

1. .... you see the doctor? That wound looks infected.
2. You .... to come in here! Entering this room is strictly forbidden.
3. What .... I do with this dog? It's driving me crazy.
4. You really .... tease your sister so much. Why can't you be nice for a change?
5. I know, I .... to know about your secret – but Mary told me.

79 ! Complete the sentences with a suitable form for *lassen*.

EXAMPLE My brother was such a jerk. When I was a child he *made* me eat worms and spiders.

1. Look! I .... my car washed today by the neighbours' children. They did a nice job, I think!
2. Simon .... not .... me use the car last weekend, Mum, but this weekend it's my turn!
3. .... the editing of the text to Ben. He's an expert at spelling.
4. .... your time. There's no need to hurry.
5. .... it, Ashley. How many times have I told you not to do that?
6. Last night we had to .... a doctor because my little sister felt sick.
7. That film always .... me cry.
8. We .... our wedding cake made by my cousin.
9. Someone has .... the front door open! It wasn't me this time.

80 ! **Open gap fill: Complete the text with a suitable modal verb. Mind tenses and forms of *lassen* and *sollen*.**

Hi Pietro,

I have just returned from New York – and I've truly left my heart in that city.

1. *Let* me tell you my story from the beginning.

Do you remember my dad promising me that I **2.** .... travel to New York if I passed my finals with good grades? Well, I **3.** .... do it, of course, and I passed with flying colours. So my dad **4.** .... keep his promise, too!

The night before the flight I **5.** .... hardly sleep because I felt so excited. I **6.** .... take my best friend Jake with me, so we picked him up early to catch the morning flight. When it was our turn to check in, we realised that we didn't have seats next to each other. We asked the flight attendant if she **7.** .... do something about it, but she said no. The prospect of spending my first 10-hour-flight without company didn't **8.** .... me feel too happy, of course, when we boarded the plane. Suddenly, a flight attendant approached us, asking, "**9.** .... we invite you to our business class?"

I **10.** .... believe my ears! But she was definitely holding two tickets in her hands. Ten minutes later, cosily snuggled into my large seat and holding a glass of champagne in my hand, I **11.** .... hardly wait for the plane to take off.

The flight was fantastic! We **12.** .... choose from a wide range of films and TV series, and the food was fantastic. My first impression of the United States, however, turned out to be quite horrible. They **13.** .... us wait for hours at the immigration counter. Then, the immigration officer took our fingerprints and photos and asked us tons of strange questions. They **14.** .... us feel like criminals. After I had claimed my luggage, I was stopped for a routine check of my suitcase. The problem was that Jake **15.** ________________ to wait for me! He had to move on without me – and it took us some time and effort to find each other again.

Hours later we finally arrived at our hotel. The moment we stepped into our room and saw the amazing view over New York's gigantic skyline, all the problems we **16.** ________________ to face at JFK were worth it. We took a long shower and fell into our comfy king-size beds. Although Jake and I had planned to go out that evening, we **17.** ________________ to lift a finger. So we made use of the room service and **18.** ________________ for burgers, steaks and fries. Yummy!

Jake and I started the next morning with a huge American breakfast: pancakes, waffles, bacon, eggs and hash browns. On our sightseeing tour afterwards we realised that we **19.** ________________ have eaten so much – it was hot and we felt lazy and stuffed. So Jake said, "Listen, Mike – if we don't want to gain too much weight we **20.** ________________ to eat less." But I answered, "Not if we do as much exercise as we already have!" And I was right! We had already visited the Empire State Building, Rockefeller Centre and Fifth Avenue. At the Abercrombie & Fitch flagship store on Fifth Avenue I even asked if I **21.** ________________ take a photo of myself and the elk … but the 'sales associate', as the assistants call themselves here, said no, sorry!

After this tour I told Jake that I **22.** ________________ relax for a while. My feet were hurting and I felt hot. So we looked for a shady spot in Central Park and dozed off for a while. I **23.** ________________ have stayed there forever – but we **24.** ________________ leave for the Lion King musical on Broadway. Pietro, if you ever have the chance of seeing this show you **25.** ________________ do it! It's the best production I have ever seen.

I'm sorry, but I **26.** ________________ stop writing now. My mother is telling me that she **27.** ________________ me use the computer tomorrow if I don't **28.** ________________ my sister use it now! I'll be back soon.

Yours, Mike

81 !! **Complete the sentences with the words in brackets.**

Lenny: Hi Donna! Sorry for being late – I **wasn't allowed to leave/couldn't leave** *(nicht dürfen – leave)* the house without finishing mowing the lawn.

Donna: No problem! I only just arrived, too. Before I left, I realised that I .... *(sollen – feed)* our dog two hours before – so I quickly gave her some tin food. But Stella ate it too quickly, threw it all up and I .... *(müssen – clean)* the kitchen floor.

Lenny: Poor you! Tell me, Donna – .... *(dürfen – you – join)* us on our skiing trip next weekend?

Donna: But you know, I .... *(müssen – hand in)* that book report on Monday. My mum says that I .... *(dürfen – come)* with you if I have finished it before the weekend.

Lenny: But that's fantastic, Donna! I have already written mine – so if you want to, I .... *(können – helfen)* you!

Donna: Cool! And if I show the report to my mum tomorrow I .... *(können – go)* on that trip. I'm so looking forward to the weekend!

Lenny: Don't forget to take your ice skates with you. The lake is frozen and we .... *(können – skate)* there!

Donna: Perfect! I .... *(nicht können – skate)* for years because it was never cold enough.

Lenny: Me neither. And you .... *(nicht müssen – take)* a sledge with you. They've got some there. So, see you this afternoon for your book report. Bye!

Donna: Thank you! Bye.

82 !! Multiple choice: Segways

You are going to read a text about Segways. Some words are missing from the text. Choose the correct answer (A, B, C or D) for each gap (1–11). Then write your answers in the space provided. The first one (0) has been done for you.

You **(0)** .... people riding it on a sightseeing tour through Paris or San Francisco. It is a strange looking device with two wheels that **(1)** .... steered with your body weight. We are talking about the Segway PT – short for Personal Transporter. The name Segway is derived from the word *segue*, which means *to move smoothly*. And that is exactly the feeling you have when riding this gadget.

So, how **(2)** .... you picture such a ride? Bear in mind – you **(3)** .... to "board" the Segway without listening carefully to the safety instructions. There is no steering wheel, accelerator or break; there's only YOU. It is only your body weight and sense of balance that steers the Segway wherever you want it to go. When you move your body to the front, the vehicle accelerates; when you move it back, it gets slower, stops, and even moves backwards. If you want to go right, lean to the right. If you want to go left – lean to the left, of course. This means that you **(4)** .... pay close attention to every move you make if you do not want to hurt yourself badly. But don't panic. At first, you **(5)** .... feel awkward or even totally unfit for the Segway, but after a few minutes you will get the hang of it. And soon, you will feel like you **(6)** .... live without this cool device ever again: Riding a Segway is highly addictive. However, you **(7)** .... get too overexcited – the Segway can reach a speed of 50 km/h. Thus, a moment of carelessness might lead to disaster.

Today, Segways are mainly used for fun, but originally, they **(8)** .... supposed to revolutionise city traffic. Dean Kamen, the inventor of the Segway, was convinced that this vehicle would thoroughly change modern private transport. In 2010, Jimi Heselden bought Segway Inc., as he was also convinced that Segways would replace cars within a few years. However, Heselden died only some months later, falling off a cliff on his Segway. Investigations revealed that Heselden's death **(9)** .... caused by his own fault.

You certainly **(10)** .... feel discouraged to drive this vehicle. Once you have mastered riding a Segway in "normal" conditions, you can even go one step ahead. There are now off-road tours on All-Terrain-Segways available. So if you feel bored with your old mountain bike, the All-Terrain-Segway **(11)** .... be an option for you.

0	A	might see	B	should see	C	*may have seen*	D	should have seen
1	A	had to be	B	should be	C	is supposed to be	D	must be
2	A	can	B	will	C	must	D	should
3	A	will be allowed	B	had	C	will have	D	won't be allowed
4	A	are allowed to	B	will have to	C	might	D	won't have to
5	A	will have to	B	ought to	C	might	D	should
6	A	can't	B	could	C	will have to	D	won't be able to
7	A	ought to	B	must not	C	don't have to	D	haven't had to
8	A	were	B	will be	C	are	D	have been
9	A	has to be	B	was to be	C	must have been	D	should have been
10	A	may not	B	must not	C	should not	D	might not
11	A	should	B	might	C	can	D	ought to

0	1	2	3	4	5	6	7	8	9	10	11
C											

PASSIVE VOICE – LEIDEFORM

A Grundsätzliches über die Leideform (das Passiv)

Aktiv und Passiv (oder Tätigkeitsform und Leideform; *active voice* und *passive voice*) zeigen an, wer etwas tut und mit wem etwas geschieht.

active voice (Tätigkeitsform)	***passive voice*** (Leideform)
das **Subjekt** des Satzes **tut etwas** – es ist **„tätig“** – es ist **„aktiv“**	mit dem **Subjekt** des Satzes **geschieht etwas** – es **„erleidet“** etwas – es ist **„passiv“**
*Workers **planted** the tree last year.* → die Arbeiter haben etwas getan	*The tree **was planted** last year.* → mit den Bäumen ist etwas passiert
Das Aktiv verwendet man eher dann, wenn der „Ausführende“ bekannt ist und genannt werden soll.	Das Passiv verwendet man eher dann, wenn der „Ausführende“ unwichtig oder unbekannt ist oder nicht genannt werden soll.
Wichtiger ist, WER etwas tut als WAS geschieht.	**Wichtig ist, WAS geschieht und nicht WER etwas tut.**
	Soll oder muss der „Ausführende“ genannt werden, verwendet man ***by + object***
*My grandfather **planted** all these trees.*	*All these trees **were planted by my grandfather**.*
Hier sprechen wir vor allem vom Großvater und nicht von den Bäumen.	Wir sprechen hier in erster Linie über die Bäume und nicht über den Opa.

B Bildung des Passivs

Die Bildung der Leideform erfolgt mit ***to be + 3rd form***.

tense	*form of "to be"*		*3rd form*
	singular	*plural*	
present simple *present progressive*	*am/is* *am/is being*	*are* *are being*	*written*
past simple *past progressive*	*was* *was being*	*were* *were being*	*sent* *closed*
present perfect simple	*have/has been*		*reported*
„will future“	*will be*		*answered*
future perfect	*will have been*		*torn down*
conditional present	*would be*		*informed*
conditional perfect	*would have been*		*repaired*
past perfect	*had been*		*taken*
infinitive	*(can, must, might …) be*		*asked*

83 Put the verbs into passive voice (present tense or past tense).

EXAMPLE All our home-exercises **are/were corrected** *(correct)* by our teachers.

1. The gaps in this exercise ______ *(fill)* with verbs in the correct tense. That's not really difficult!
2. Can you tell me, when this house ______ *(build)*? It looks very old and romantic.
3. The new *Passenger* CD with its hit "Let Her Go" ______ *(download)* 20,000 times last week.
4. Usually all the shopping ______ *(do)* by my mum. I quite like that. But when my dad goes shopping, the cupboards ______ *(fill)* with cookies and cakes. Yummy!
5. Tell me, Paula, why ______ *(you/not invite)* to Jessica's birthday party last Saturday? I thought you liked each other!
6. Why ______ *(I/not inform)* about the change of plan? Don't you think that this is unfair?
7. Sarah has difficulties doing her English homework because the new grammar aspect ______ *(explain)* very badly by Mrs Shockhead, their teacher.
8. I have no idea who paid the bill for my double cheeseburger and fries, but it ______ *(not pay)* by me! I'm sure about that!
9. David's message to Nora ______ *(not answer)*, so he felt very sad and worried.
10. The new Sony Xperia smart phone ______ *(advertise)* on TV. It really looks cool.
11. The maths test ______ *(not announce)* by the teacher in time, so most of the class got low grades or even failed it.
12. Every year, thousands of patents ______ *(register)* in our country.
13. They say that last week, lots of letters ______ *(lose)* in the post, but they don't know how this could happen!

C passive progressive

Passive progressive drückt aus, was **jetzt gerade** oder **zu einem vergangenen Zeitpunkt** gerade geschieht oder geschah. Diese Form gibt es nur in *present* und *past*.

Die Bildung erfolgt mit ***to be + being + 3rd form***.

present	*The doors* ***are being closed****!* → Die Türen werden (jetzt gerade!) geschlossen.
	Be careful! The house ***is being watched****!* → Das Haus wird (eben jetzt) beobachtet.
	Why ***am*** *I* ***being stopped****, officer? I didn't do anything!* → Warum werde ich (in diesem Augenblick) aufgehalten?
past	*Just as we arrived, the lights* ***were being turned*** *off.* → Gerade als wir eintrafen, wurden die Lichter abgedreht.
	When I looked out of the window, my car ***was being towed*** *away.* → Als ich aus dem Fenster sah, wurde mein Auto eben abgeschleppt.

D ! passive infinitive

Die Bildung erfolgt mit ***modal verb + be + 3rd form***.

can / cannot	*This behaviour* ***cannot be tolerated****.*
could / could not	*The explosion* ***could be heard*** *all over town.*
may / may not	*We* ***may be invited*** *to Jeremy's party next week.*
might / might not	*All flights* ***might be cancelled*** *because of the storm.*
must / must not	*No details* ***must be leaked*** *to the media!*
should / should not	*Bicycles* ***should not be left*** *outside overnight.*
need not	*Certain flowers* ***need not be watered*** *every day.*

E ! „man"-Sätze – Das Passiv in „neutralen" Aussagen

believe	***It is believed*** *that Tiger Woods will be making a comeback.* ***Tiger Woods is believed*** *to be making a comeback.* → Man glaubt/nimmt an, dass Tiger Woods …
expect	***It is expected*** *that no one will survive this terrible fire.* ***No one is expected*** *to survive this terrible fire.* → Man erwartet, dass niemand dieses … Feuer überleben wird.
say	***It is said*** *that Harry knows more about magic than anyone else.* ***Harry is said*** *to know more about magic than anyone else.* → Man sagt, Harry wisse mehr über Zauberei als …
think	***It is thought*** *that ManU will win the next Champions League.* ***ManU is thought*** *to win the next Champions League.* → Man nimmt an (denkt), ManU werde … gewinnen.
know	***It is known*** *that many athletes pray before a competition.* ***Many athletes are known*** *to pray before a competition.* → Man weiß, dass viele Sportler vor einem Wettbewerb beten.

84 ! Match the sentences by writing the numbers in the boxes.

1.	The lights were switched off	A	done by the students themselves.
2.	The car looks dirty. It	B	the money had been sent.
3.	The test papers are being	C	into the stadium right now.
4.	The laptop can be	D	downloaded illegally.
5.	Films have often been	E	after the last customer had left.
6.	The Olympic torch is being carried	F	used any time. Just take it!
7.	The flat was bought after	G	corrected at the moment.
8.	All exercises must be	H	should be washed again.

1	2	3	4	5	6	7	8
E							

85 !! Translate the sentences, mind the correct tense.

EXAMPLE Das Geschirr sollte von uns abgewaschen werde.
The dishes should be done by us.

1. Die Blumen werden jetzt gerade gegossen.

2. Während ich nach Hause ging, wurde ich von ein paar Leuten aufgehalten.

3. Das Word-Dokument wurde gerade eben ausgedruckt.

4. Man weiß, dass Rauchen schädlich ist.

86 ! Circle the correct option.

During the last few weeks I *wouldn't be reached* / *couldn't be reached* on my mobile phone because I spent some time in the African savanna. I actually didn't know that I would travel there as the flight *is booked* / *had been booked* without my knowledge. So I was really surprised! However, during my stay there it rained heavily; our camp *was almost flooded* / *is almost flooded* and many wild animals *are drowned* / *were drowned* by the water. It was quite dangerous, but such a fantastic experience *shall be had* / *should be had* by everybody one day!

F ! Aktiv oder Passiv?

Man kann einen Sachverhalt aktiv oder passiv ausdrücken.

Aktiv → *The dog* ***bit*** *the postman.*
Die Handlung des Hundes **steht im Mittelpunkt**.

Passiv → *The postman* ***was bitten*** *by the dog.*
Das Schicksal des Briefträgers **steht im Mittelpunkt**.

THE POSTMAN WAS BITTEN BY THE DOG.

THE DOG BIT THE POSTMAN.

Damit man einen Sachverhalt sowohl passiv als auch aktiv ausdrücken kann, muss man die folgenden Regeln beachten:

Regel 1: *active to passive*

Our dog	***bit***	***the postman***.
S	P	O
The postman	***was bitten***	***by our dog***.

- Das aktive Objekt *(the postman)* wird zum passiven Subjekt.
- Das aktive Prädikat wird zum passiven Prädikat; es teilt sich in die entsprechende Form von „*to be*“+ *3rd form (bit* → *was bitten)*.
- Das aktive Subjekt *(our dog)* wird nur dann zum passiven Objekt, wenn es dabei um **jemand Bestimmten** geht und der passive Satz ohne Nennung des Objekts nicht vollständig wäre. Es wird mit *by* an den Satz gebunden → „*by-object*“.

Regel 2: *passive to active*

The postman	***was taken***	–	*to hospital.*
S	P	O	
They/We	***took***	***the postman***	*to hospital.*

- Wenn der passive Satz kein *by-object* aufweist, wählt man ein neutrales aktives Subjekt (meist *they*, aber auch *people* oder *you*).
Wenn es ein *by-object* gibt, wird es zum aktiven Subjekt. (Siehe Regel 1)
- Das passive Prädikat *(was taken)* wird zum aktiven Prädikat *(took)*. Es verliert dabei die Form von „*to be*“, und das Verb wird an die entsprechende Zeitstufe angepasst.
- Das passive Subjekt *(the postman)* wird zum aktiven Objekt.

87 Are the sentences active (A) or passive (P)?

EXAMPLE My car was taken to the garage, so I came by bike. P

1. Somebody has just knocked on the door but I don't know who. ______
2. I have been interested in Star Wars films for a long time. ______
3. After the joke about blonds had been told, nobody laughed. ______
4. This book is surely going to be made into a film. ______
5. *The Big Bang Theory* has always been my favourite series. ______

88 !! Change the active sentences into passive ones and the other way round. Leave out the by-object where necessary.

EXAMPLE They installed iTunes on this laptop before they sold it.
iTunes was installed on this laptop before it was sold.

1. After a long walk I had to clean my dog's paws.

______

2. I was given this mobile phone by my best friend Tina.

______

3. Honestly, they have never shown so much nonsense on TV before.

______

4. People claim that enough sleep makes you look young and beautiful.

______

5. Our homework must definitely be handed in today.

______

6. Somebody ought to call the police before more terrible things happen!

______

7. The students' answers must be written on an extra sheet.

______

8. Don't forget that people speak English here!

______

9. Listen, they are mowing the lawn again.

______

89 !! Put the verbs into active or passive voice (all tenses!).

EXAMPLE Austrian ski racer Marcel Hirscher **has been admired** *(admire)* by thousands of fans for a long time because he is a great skier and a very nice guy.

1. Severe punishment .... *(must carry out)* after a serious crime because otherwise a deterrent effect .... *(cannot achieve)*.
2. *Pink's* live act in Vienna last year .... *(see)* by a large crowd. All of them .... *(cheer)* enthusiastically when the queen of pop came onto the stage.
3. My dad finally bought the new BMW which he .... *(fall)* in love with ages ago. Now he .... *(seem)* to be the happiest man alive. It's funny because the old car .... *(be)* always dirty but the new one .... *(polish)* and cleaned nearly every other day.
4. I have to confess that I .... *(fall)* in love recently. I .... *(meet)* the guy at the theatre a few weeks ago when *Romeo & Juliet* .... *(perform)*. We .... *(see)* each other regularly since then and millions of messages and emails .... *(send)* in both directions.
5. Usually our classroom's blackboard .... *(clean)* by Jimmy, but this week I .... *(do)* it because Jimmy is ill and .... *(have)* to stay at home.
6. Last week it .... *(snow)* so much that even now most trees .... *(cover)* in white.
7. .... *(you/ever/tell)* that it's impolite to speak with a full mouth? You must really work on your manners!
8. If we don't go to Joe's birthday party this year, we .... *(not invite)* again.
9. By now I should .... *(unterstand)* the passive.

G !! Sätze mit zwei Objekten

Manche Sätze haben zwei Objekte – ein **Personalobjekt** und ein **Sachobjekt**. Anders als im Deutschen können im Englischen beide zum Subjekt eines passiven Satzes werden.

	Person	Sache
They asked	***us***	***many silly questions.***
They will show	***you***	***some very strange things.***
Someone gave	***Jake***	***the wrong address.***

Im modernen Alltagsenglisch kommt das ***personal passive*** sehr häufig vor – im Deutschen ist das gar nicht möglich:

We	***were asked***	*many silly questions.*
Some very strange things	***will be shown***	*to you.*
Jake	***was given***	*the wrong address.*

H ! Passiv mit *phrasal verbs (verb + preposition)*

Die Verbindung ***verb*** + ***preposition*** darf man im Passiv **nicht trennen**.

*You must **fill in** all empty spaces.* → *All empty spaces **must be filled in**.*
*They've **turned down** my application.* → *My application **has been turned down**.*
*They **put out** the fire very quickly.* → *The fire **was put out** very quickly.*

ask out	zum Essen einladen	***look up***	nachschlagen
blow up	sprengen	***make up***	erfinden
break into	einbrechen	***mix up***	verwechseln
bring up	erwähnen	***pay for***	bezahlen
call off	absagen	***pick up***	mitnehmen
care for	versorgen, betreuen	***point out***	hinweisen
clean up	aufräumen	***put down***	schlecht machen
close down	zusperren	***put off***	verschieben
cross out	durchstreichen	***put out***	(Feuer) löschen
cut down	umschneiden	***put together***	zusammenstellen
fill in	ausfüllen, einsetzen	***run over***	überfahren
find out	herausfinden	***send back***	zurückschicken
give away	verschenken	***switch on/off***	ein-/ausschalten
hand out	austeilen	***take apart***	auseinandernehmen
hold back	zurückhalten	***take back***	zurückbringen
knock out	niederschlagen	***take off***	ausziehen
let down	im Stich lassen	***tear up***	zerreißen
look after	sorgen für	***throw away***	wegwerfen
look at	betrachten	***turn down***	ablehnen
look for	suchen	***turn on/off***	an-/abdrehen
look into	untersuchen	***use up***	aufbrauchen

90 ! Form two passive voice sentences.

EXAMPLE They gave Captain Farris the Medal of Honour for extraordinary bravery.
Captain Farris was given the Medal of Honour for extraordinary bravery.
The Medal of Honour was given to Captain Farris for extraordinary bravery.

1. Someone sent Sebastian some nasty emails last week.

   ____

   ____

2. They will serve the new guests welcome drinks in the hotel lobby.

   ____

   ____

3. We have mailed Mr Cooper all the documents.

   ____

   ____

4. The Duke himself was showing the tourists the portrait gallery.

   ____

   ____

91 !! Complete the sentences with passive and phrasal verbs. Mind the use of the correct tense.

EXAMPLE Usually babies *are cared for* (*sorgen für*) by their parents.

1. Because of the wet and foggy weather lots of national and international flights ______________________ (*absagen*) recently.
2. Last night's fire ______________________ (*löschen*) by the brave firemen. Luckily nobody was hurt.
3. The chocolate muffins ______________________ (*bezahlen müssen*) at the cashier's desk. One is $ 1.20.
4. The shower gel ______________________ (*aufbrauchen*), so now I must go to the chemist's shop and buy a new one.
5. All the T-shirts ______________________ (*mussten, zurückschicken*) because they were the wrong size and colour.

92 !! Complete the letter with suitable verbs in active or passive voice. Again, mind the correct use of the tenses.

Hi Leo,

Guess what!! I'm here at the Neusiedlersee in Burgenland, Austria, and it's just great! You know I ***have always wanted*** *(immer schon wollen)* to spend some time in Austria, and here I am. I ______________ *(ankommen)* on Wednesday last week, and so far we ______________ *(tun/machen)* some great sightseeing. We ______________ *(sehen)* St. Stephen's Cathedral in Vienna and I also went to the Prater. But then Vanessa had a brilliant idea and so our plans ______________ *(verändern/abändern)* spontaneously. We travelled to Neusiedlersee as none of us ______________ *(jemals/sein)* there before. Now we ______________ *(bleiben)* at a little cottage in a village that ______________ *(nennen/heißen)* Podersdorf. It's fun here, really!

Anyway, yesterday was the best and most exciting day! We went kitesurfing. ______________ *(du/jemals/hören)* about it? Early in the morning we went to a kite and windsurf school where boards can ______________ *(mieten)*. We ______________ *(auch/geben)* all the necessary equipment, and afterwards the whole stuff ______________ *(tragen)* over to the lake by Günther, our instructor. He was quite nice, by the way ... ;-)

To cut a long story short, kitesurfing is REALLY difficult and challenging. When there's a strong wind, the kite has so much power that you ______________ *(schleifen/zerren)* through the water all the time. That's quite exhausting. But at the end of the day, we ______________ *(schaffen)* to ride some waves and we were happy with our performance! So maybe we ______________ *(mieten)* the boards again tomorrow!

Love, Sonja ☺

93 !! Multiple choice: A Trip to Normandy

You are going to read a text about Etretat, a little village in France. Some words are missing from the text. Choose the correct answer (A, B, C or D) for each gap (1–10). Then write your answers in the space provided. The first one (0) has been done for you.

A Trip to Normandy

Hi, I'm Sophia Steel. I am 33 years old and I **(0)** ______ for a travel magazine called *Travel On*. Usually my boss sends me off to rocky, mountainous areas to check them out and to write interesting articles about whether or not I liked it there. My most spectacular trip was definitely reviewing the ascent of Mont Blanc in 2010. That was what I call a real adventure. I **(1)** ______ my job because I simply love the mountains. A few weeks ago, however, one of my colleagues fell ill all of a sudden, so I **(2)** ______ take over her job and write a traveller's review of a little village in Normandy. Its name is Etretat, and as I had not even heard about this place before but knew that there would be sea instead of mountains, I **(3)** ______ not very happy.

But of course I **(4)** ______ a choice so I packed my stuff and left for France. I also took my little dictionary and a booklet called *French for Tourists* with me, as I last spoke French when I was at school. The journey was okay and it didn't take long. At the airport I hired a little Peugeot 206, consulted my newly-acquired road map and made my way to Etretat. The drive took about two hours, during which I passed by numerous cornfields and cow pastures. Even though I was at first not amused to have been sent there, I have to confess that upon my arrival in Etretat I was simply fascinated, amazed and overwhelmed.

(5) ______ a small fishing village originally, Etretat is today best known for its cliffs that stretch for several kilometres along the coastline. In earlier times these cliffs, including three natural arches, attracted painters and artists like Eugène Boudin, Gustave Courbet or Claude Monet. Today it's mostly tourists that visit Etretat for its natural beauty. But there is also a big number of Parisians who make daytrips to the coast or travel there for the weekend. The local inhabitants, however, don't really like them as they are sometimes very snotty and snobbish.

After I **(6)** ______ into my small apartment, I took my camera and my iPad and made my way towards the cliffs. They were very easy to find – I only had to follow a meadow path and could not really miss them. You can then walk along the top of the coastline, constantly watching the grey-white stone formations, and above them you can see an indefinite number of graceful sea-gulls soaring high in the air. They **(7)** ______ funny and cute noises when they communicate with each other, and I stopped and enjoyed listening to them. You can spend hours simply listening and watching and that's exactly what I **(8)** ______. And you never get bored of the sight of the water moving towards the beach with its rock formations, and away from it again.

I spent the next days exploring the surroundings, discovering little villages and cities. I strolled along narrow streets, drank *Caffé Latte* and ate a vast number of chocolate croissants and tasty baguettes. I **(9)** ______ whether I gained weight or not, I simply enjoyed life and everything it offered to me during those few days. You also get used to the French lifestyle fast and you soon **(10)** ______ the unhurried and stress-free way of life of the French. It was great! But soon – I'm tempted to say too soon – I had to pack my suitcase again. I took a last look at the breathtaking scenery, smelled the Atlantic Ocean for the last time, and started my journey back home, giving special thanks to my sick colleague in my mind …

0	A	shall work	B	*work*	C	worked	D	will work
1	A	am loving	B	have loved	C	love	D	loved
2	A	will have to	B	must	C	has to	D	had to
3	A	am	B	have been	C	was	D	had been
4	A	didn't have	B	didn't had	C	doesn't have	D	haven't had
5	A	having been	B	beeing	C	being	D	been
6	A	have checked	B	checked	C	had checked	D	was checking
7	A	are making	B	were making	C	made	D	make
8	A	am doing	B	did do	C	did	D	had done
9	A	haven't cared	B	didn't care	C	didn't cared	D	not cared
10	A	didn't take up	B	do take up	C	took up	D	take up

0	1	2	3	4	5	6	7	8	9	10
B										

94 ! Change the active sentences into passive ones.

EXAMPLE Usually my boss sends me off to rocky areas.
Usually I am sent off to rocky areas (by my boss).

1. They published a story about the ascent of Mont Blanc in 2010.

2. I had to take over my colleague's job.

3. After I had prepared everything, I left for France.

4. In the past, these cliffs attracted painters and artists.

5. Today, mostly tourists visit Etretat.

6. You can see the grey-white stone formations from everywhere.

7. Visitors will soon take up the unhurried way of life of the French.

PRESENT PARTICIPLE – MITTELWORT DER GEGENWART

A Grundsätzliches zu *present participle*

- *Present participle* ist auch bekannt als 1. Mittelwort, Mittelwort der Gegenwart oder Partizipium Präsens.
- *Present participle* ist eine **„ing-form“**, die Bildung erfolgt mit ***infinitive* + *ing***.

ACHTUNG RECHTSCHREIBUNG!

- **Wegfall** des „stummen e“ am Wortende: *take* → *taking*
- **Verdopplung** des Endkonsonanten: *stop* → *stopping*
- **Wandlung** von -ie zu -y bei: *lie* → *lying; die* → *dying; tie* → *tying*

B Verwendung

B1 Teil von *progressive form*, die Bildung erfolgt mit *to be* + *present participle*.

*We **are waiting**. – The baby **was crying**. – It **has been raining** hard.*

B2 Als Adjektiv zur näheren Beschreibung eines Nomens (Hauptwort, *noun*)

*a **shooting** star – an **interesting** story – “**Sitting** Bull”*

B3 Nach bestimmten Verben

- **nicht zwingend** nach **see – watch – hear – feel – notice** für einzelne, nicht wiederholte Handlungen
  *How long have you been here? I didn't **see** you **coming** in!*
  *I've **noticed** three men **climbing** in through that window!*
- **zwingend** nach **go – come – keep – quit – catch**
  *Do you ever **go skiing** in summer?*
  *The firefighters **came running** up the stairs, **breathing** heavily.*
  *Why do you **keep looking** at me so foolishly?*
  ***Quit fooling** around, Joe, and be serious.*
  *You'll never again **catch** me **asking** those people a favour!*

95 ! **Complete the sentences with either the infinitive or present participle form of the verbs in brackets. Sometimes you may have to use full present, present perfect or past progressive forms.**

EXAMPLE Oh, have you been here all the time? I didn't notice you **sitting** *(sit)* here when I came in.

1. I sometimes hear my cat Frankie .... *(cry)* loudly outside the garden door when he is too lazy to use the cat flap.
2. Do you often go .... *(skate)* to the park?
3. Look at our dog! She is watching the baby rabbits .... *(play)* in their cage. How cute!
4. I don't know what to do with our cat Minki. Every day when I come home from school I catch her .... *(sleep)* on the dinner table!
5. I've tried to quit .... *(smoke)* several times, but I always fail.
6. I often watch my baby brother .... *(sleep)* peacefully in his bed. It's such a cute sight.
7. Monica, where have you been? I .... *(wait)* for you for twenty minutes.
8. Keep .... *(try)*, Laura, and soon you'll manage to do this exercise without help.
9. Yesterday, when I came into my room, I saw that my little brother .... *(hop)* up and down on my bed! When he saw me, he just grinned and ran out of my room.
10. Last time I saw Beatrice, I noticed her .... *(look)* rather sad. So I asked her, but she said she was alright.
11. Sorry, Cindy. I can't talk to you now. I have to watch my little sister .... *(take)* her bath. I'll call you later.
12. Look! This man .... *(try)* to break into the shop.

B4 ! Anstelle eines einschränkenden Relativsatzes *(defining relative clause)*

People who work *in coal mines often suffer from "black lung".*
People working *in coal mines often suffer from "black lung".*
We saw lots of bats ***that were hanging*** *from the ceiling of the cave.*
We saw lots of bats ***hanging*** *from the ceiling of the cave.*
(Mehr Informationen im Kapitel *relative clauses* ab Seite 104.)

B5 ! Anstelle eines Gliedsatzes mit *after, as, when* oder *while*

- Zwingend bei Einleitung mit ***while***
  → **gleiches Subjekt in Hauptsatz und Gliedsatz** (S = S)

While ***we*** *were driving through Scotland,* ***we*** *saw lots of sheep.*
Driving *through Scotland,* ***we*** *saw lots of sheep.*

- Bei Einleitung mit ***after, as, because*** oder ***when***
  → **verschiedene Subjekte in Hauptsatz und Gliedsatz** möglich (S ≠ S)

present participle muss am Beginn des Satzes stehen.

S = S
When ***I*** *was leaving the train station,* ***I*** *saw it was raining.*
Leaving *the train station,* ***I*** *saw it was raining.*
As ***we*** *had enough money left,* ***we*** *decided to take a taxi home.*
Having *enough money left,* ***we*** *decided to take a taxi home.*

S ≠ S
After ***the tourists*** *had gone,* ***the natives*** *could relax again.*
The tourists having *gone,* ***the natives*** *could relax again.*
When ***the show*** *was over,* ***we*** *all went to a bar together.*
The show being *over,* ***we*** *all went to a bar together.*

B6 ! Zur Verknüpfung und/oder Verkürzung von Sätzen

Unter zwei Bedingungen:

- die Handlungen finden **gleichzeitig** oder **knapp hintereinander** statt
- alle Handlungen haben **das gleiche Subjekt**

Die „Haupthandlung" bleibt unverändert, die „Nebenhandlung" wird durch *present participle* ausgedrückt.

Julia *was walking to school.* ***She*** *was listening to her iPad.*

(a) ***Walking*** *to school,* ***Julia*** *was listening to her iPad.*
▼ „Nebenhandlung" ▼ „Haupthandlung"

(b) ***Julia*** *was walking to school* ***listening*** *to her iPad.*
▼ „Haupthandlung" ▼ „Nebenhandlung"

96 ! Rewrite the relative clause sentences. Use present participle forms.

EXAMPLE We saw a lot of people who swam in the lake.
We saw a lot of people swimming in the lake.

1. Passengers who sit in rows 25 to 35 can board the plane now.

2. Police caught three men who were driving a stolen car.

3. Animals that live in cold climates usually hibernate.

97 !! Rewrite the sentences if possible. Use present participle forms.

EXAMPLE While I was waiting for the school bus, I realised that I had forgotten my lunch pack.
Waiting for the school bus, I realised I had forgotten my lunch pack.

1. Mum was cooking dinner while Dad was looking after my brother.

2. After the teacher had left the classroom, the pupils started to cheer.

3. As I had bought enough food, I invited all my friends for dinner.

4. As my friends were staying for dinner, I had to buy lots of food.

RELATIVE CLAUSES – RELATIVSÄTZE

A Grundsätzliches über Relativsätze

Ein Relativsatz ist **ein Nebensatz, der ein Satzglied erweitert und/oder näher erklärt**. Er wird durch ein bezügliches Fürwort (Relativpronomen; ***relative pronoun***) eingeleitet, das den Bezug zu dem Satzglied herstellt:

Do you know ***the people who*** *have bought the house next door?*

- ***who*** leitet den Relativsatz ein
- ***who*** bezieht sich auf „*the people*", die damit näher bezeichnet werden

B *relative pronouns*

who – whom – whose – which – that – where – when

who, whom

- beziehen sich auf Personen (*who* = Subjekt; *whom* = Objekt)
- *whom* wird heute oft durch *who* ersetzt

Teachers who *are strict are not always popular.*
Mr Myers, who(m) *I like a lot, can be very strict.*

whose

- weist auf den 2. Fall *(genitive)* hin und drückt Besitz aus
- kann sich auf Personen und Sachen beziehen

Are you ***the student whose*** *parents have just called?*
This is ***the car whose*** *driver has disappeared.*

which

- bezieht sich auf Sachen (wird in *defining relative clauses* oft durch „*that*" ersetzt (siehe Punkt C);
- kann sich auf einen ganzen Satz beziehen

The house which *collapsed yesterday was very old.*
(besser: ***The house that*** *collapsed yesterday* …)
This is the pen without which I can't write the test.
Gordon called the police, ***which*** *was a clever idea.*

that

- kommt nur in *defining relative clauses* vor (siehe Punkt C)
- kann sich auf Personen und Sachen beziehen, einzeln oder gemeinsam
- wird verwendet, wenn das Bezugswort ein Superlativ *(best, fastest …)* oder ein „Extremwort" *(first, last, only, nothing, everything …)* ist

I took lots of photos of ***the cowboys that (who)*** *rode in the rodeo.*
I took lots of photos of ***the horses that (which)*** *came into the arena.*
It was ***the best*** *thing* ***that*** *could happen to us.*

where (örtlich)
This is the place ***where*** we first met.

when (zeitlich)
That was the time ***when*** we met.

98 Fill in the fitting relative pronoun.

EXAMPLE Last holiday I met a boy *who (that)* was totally awesome.

1. This is the girl .... dog bit me yesterday.
2. Tom offered me a birthday present, ... really surprised me.
3. Look! There is the girl with .... I had that great date.
4. Sandra Higgs, ... speaks four languages, got the job.
5. The Thames, ... runs through London, is a famous river.
6. How was the test .... you had to sit yesterday?
7. That's the worst essay .... has ever been written.
8. This house is everything .... we have ever dreamed of.
9. Is this the street .... your granny lives?
10. Where can I see the picture .... won first prize?

99 ! Combine the sentences into one by using the correct relative pronoun.

EXAMPLE We went to a beach. It was absolutely beautiful.
We went to a beach that (which) was absolutely beautiful.

1. I married the man. He was my first love.

   ....

2. Did you speak with the woman? I hit her car yesterday.

   ....

3. Please call all the clients. We've got appointments with them tomorrow.

   ....

4. I bought a new smartphone. It can be controlled without being touched.

   ....

5. My friend Tina moved to Australia last year. I had a huge crush on her.

   ....

   ....

C ! Einschränkende und erweiternde Relativsätze

einschränkende Relativsätze *defining relative clauses*	erweiternde Relativsätze *non-defining relative clauses*
Sie **schränken** die Zahl der Möglichkeiten auf einen bestimmten Fall **ein**.	Sie **erweitern** unser Wissen, indem sie zusätzliche Informationen bieten.
Sie **sind** für das vollkommene Verstehen des Satzes **nötig**.	Sie **sind** für das Verstehen des Satzes **nicht erforderlich**.
Der Relativsatz **folgt ohne Komma** (Beistrich) auf das Bezugswort.	Der Relativsatz **wird durch Kommas** vom Bezugswort **getrennt**.
People ***who live at high altitudes*** *have more red blood cells*.	*Sherpas*, ***who live at high altitudes***, *have more red blood cells*.
Everybody ***who saves the lives of others*** *is a hero*.	*My cousin Marion*, ***who saved the life of her sister***, *is a hero*.
The Louvre was the first museum ***that we visited in Paris***.	*First we visited the Louvre*, ***which is the most famous museum in Paris***.
▼ Die unterstrichenen Sätze für sich ergeben nicht viel Sinn. Erst die fett gedruckten Sätze tun dies, weil sie die Zahl der Möglichkeiten auf bestimmte Menschen oder Plätze einschränken.	▼ Die unterstrichenen Sätze sind klar verständlich, ausreichend und ergeben Sinn. Die fett gedruckten Sätze bieten nur zusätzliche Informationen, die wir aber für das Verstehen der Aussage nicht benötigen.

D !! contact clauses – Relativsätze ohne Relativpronomen

Wenn sich ein Relativsatz auf das Objekt bezieht, braucht man nicht unbedingt ein Relativpronomen.
Der Relativsatz steht in unmittelbarem Kontakt mit dem Bezugswort – daher die Bezeichnung *contact clause*.

This is the song ***that/which*** *I like best.*
→ *This is the song* ♥ *I like best.*

The girls ***that/who*** *I met at your party were fascinating.*
→ *The girls* ♥ *I met at your party were fascinating.*

Here are the pictures ***that/which*** *we took at the concert.*
→ *Here are the pictures* ♥ *we took at the concert.*

Do you remember the people with ***whom*** *we spoke last night?*
→ *Do you remember the people* ♥ *we spoke with last night?*

100 ! Defining or non-defining relative clause?

Tick whether the underlined relative clause must be set in commas or not.	yes	no
EXAMPLE London which is the capital of England is my favourite city.	X	
1. The boy with whom I had a date yesterday was a jerk.		
2. My brother who lives in Sydney will get married in June.		
3. The Eiffel Tower which we visited yesterday was crowded.		
4. Another reason that I would like to mention is poverty.		
5. My dad is the only person that I can tell everything.		
6. Do you know that guy over there who is staring at us?		
7. Mrs Jenkins who works in accounting invited me for dinner.		
8. David Beckham who earned millions with football has ended his career.		
9. I often remember our wedding which was my greatest day.		
10. Do you like the present that I gave you for Christmas?		

101 ! Contact clauses.

Tick whether the underlined relative pronoun can be omitted or not.	yes	no
EXAMPLE Mr Mathews is the teacher who gave me an A in maths.		X
1. Don't forget to put on the perfume that I sent you.		
2. That was the greatest party that I have ever been to.		
3. Where is that boy whose glue ran all over my books?		
4. I really love the dress which you bought for me.		
5. Is Jenna the girl who you forgot to invite to the party?		
6. "Cinderella" is the worst musical that I have ever seen.		
7. Can you introduce me to that boy who you've just talked to?		
8. This is the book that won countless awards and prizes.		
9. Is this the vase that almost fell and broke?		

102 !! Spot the mistake.

Tick the correct sentences. Correct the wrong ones.

EXAMPLE The film, which we saw yesterday, was a dubbed version. → *wrong*
correct: The film (that/which) we saw yesterday was a dubbed version.

1. I really don't like what you are saying about my new hairstyle.

2. I am looking for someone which can help me with my homework.

3. Love is all what I need in life.

4. My dog died last month, which still hurts.

5. Paris, which I love very much, is the most often visited city in Europe.

6. Susan is the greatest friend which you can imagine.

7. I last saw Jim in January, where I was skiing in Salzburg.

8. Jeremy is the boy with who I had a really good time in school.

9. That cake is the most extraordinary thing which I have ever tasted.

10. Mark Knopfler, whose latest CD I've just bought, is a terrific guitarist.

11. I got an A on my last English test, which really surprised me.

103 !! Combine the sentences into one. Mind relative pronouns and commas.

EXAMPLE Yesterday I ate a burger. It was the best burger I had ever tasted.
Yesterday I ate the best burger that I had ever tasted. Yesterday I ate a burger which/that was the best (that) I had ever tasted. (superlative: that)

1. Sue made up with her boyfriend again. She had been cheated on by him several times.

2. My aunt invited me to spend a month with her. She lives in Melbourne.
   (extra information: I've got two aunts.)

3. My granny always pinches my cheek when she sees me. I hate that.

4. Do you see that tree over there? Mike proposed to me there.

5. I lost my earrings. I got them from my parents.

6. Samantha finally apologised to her friend Mary. Samantha had told lies about Mary.

7. Smoking costs a lot of money. This is another fact I want to mention.

8. Do you remember the day? You told me that you loved me.

9. I've made the biggest mistake. It was buying Facebook shares.

10. Pancakes must be made with milk. They are my favourite dessert.

104 !! Multiple choice: Smovey?!?

You are going to read an article about a new invention that might help a lot of people improve their health. Some words are missing from the text. Choose the correct answer (A, B, C or D) for each gap (1–10). Then write your answers in the space provided. The first one (0) has been done for you.

Swing. Move. Smile. The word **(0)** ___ you get when you combine those three into one is: SMOVEY. But what is this thing **(1)** ___ we are talking about here? Basically, it is a new gadget that helps you lose weight and stay fit. A smovey is a small green tube twisted into a circle and filled with four metal balls. You grab two smoveys, hold them in your hands and there you go: you swing them, you move the way you want to, and you will automatically start to smile.

The smovey, **(2)** ___ was invented by Johann "Salzhans" Salzwimmer, is not only a fun device, but it also guarantees effective exercise. When you swing your arms rhythmically, the four balls start swinging at a frequency of 60 Hz – a movement **(3)** ___ can be felt all over your body. As the balls move at such a high frequency, their initial weight of half a kilo turns out to have the effect of a five kilo barbell **(4)** ___ is quite impressive. You may not realise the actual effort while you are swinging those green tubes – but you are definitely going to feel their effect the next day.

So, who is the man **(5)** ___ invention has already improved the lives of thousands of people? Johann Salzwimmer **(6)** ___ calls himself "Salzhans", is a man with a mission. In 1996 the keen skier and tennis player received the devastating news **(7)** ___ would change his life: he was suffering from Parkinson's disease! But instead of giving up on his active old life, Hans started to work on a device **(8)** ___ would help him and others to keep or regain their mobility: the smovey.

It took ten years to turn his idea into a product. With the help of investors and good friends, Johann Salzwimmer has now created an international company **(9)** ___ offers jobs in production as well as training. What's more, many of the workers **(10)** ___ Salzwimmer employs are part of a programme that helps handicapped people find jobs and earn a living.

So, if you feel like swinging, join a course. You won't regret it – I promise.

0	A	what	B	*that*	C	who	D	how
1	A	that	B	what	C	who	D	whose
2	A	that	B	–	C	what	D	which
3	A	what	B	–	C	that	D	where
4	A	that	B	, what	C	which	D	, which
5	A	whom	B	, whose	C	, whom	D	whose
6	A	who	B	, who	C	that	D	, that
7	A	, that	B	, who	C	that	D	what
8	A	that	B	, that	C	, which	D	whose
9	A	where	B	that	C	, which	D	who
10	A	of which	B	which	C	whose	D	–

0	1	2	3	4	5	6	7	8	9	10
B										

105 !! Editing: The History of the Hamburger

You are going to read a text about the history of the hamburger. In some of the lines there is a word that should not be there. Find it and write it down in the spaces provided. Some lines are okay. Indicate these with a ✔. Also, fill in a relative pronoun (who/which/that/whose) where necessary. The first ones (00, 0) have been done for you.

The History of the Hamburger

It is something ***that*** we have all eaten and enjoyed more than (00) ✔
once: a good and fresh hamburger. Most of us **all** love the smell, (0) all
the taste and not the texture of it and as a rule most of us (1) __________
consume too many of hamburgers. (2) __________
The hamburger **(1)** __________ we know and do love today is an (3) __________
American invention, but whereas the true identity of its creator is (4) __________
still unknown. There is no doubt, however, that the first type of (5) __________
hamburger goes back to the first middle of the 19th century, when (6) __________
chopped beef was a popular dish in Germany's at Hamburg. (7) __________
Rumour has it that German emigrants **(2)** __________ left for the (8) __________
United States brought on this trend to New York City. There the (9) __________
hamburger soon gained its popularity as it was filling and could (10) __________
easily be eaten while being walking or standing. Soon variations of (11) __________
the hamburger have came up and cheese, for example, was added (12) __________
to the burger in the mid-1920s. (13) __________
At that time the hamburger was primarily a food for the workmen, (14) __________
(3) __________ lunch breaks usually didn't last very long. So the (15) __________
hamburger was often served in small diners near all factories and (16) __________
could be consumed in no time even. It's probably from these little (17) __________
diners that the fast food chains **(4)** __________ we know today (18) __________
developed. We all know, of course, that the three most largest and (19) __________
most important chains today are McDonalds, Burger King and (20) __________
Wendy's. According to Wikipedia, McDonalds, **(5)** __________ (21) __________
serves 68 million people every day, can be found in 119 countries. (22) __________
It's worth mentioning of, though, that in size, appearance and (23) __________
taste the burgers don't all differ – no matter where you eat them. (24) __________
This is due to the fact that they are hardly mass-produced in (25) __________
factories, frozen and then delivered to the individual restaurants. (26) __________
The typical American hamburgers are very round but there is one (27) __________
fast food chain **(6)** __________ sells square-cut burgers: Wendy's. (28) __________
Nowadays hamburgers are served with any lettuce, bacon, tomato, (29) __________
onion, pickles, cheese and condiments like mustard, mayonnaise (30) __________
or ketchup. The burger is always grilled because when burgers **(7)** (31) __________
__________ are raw may contain of harmful bacteria. So what (32) __________
about you? Are you someone **(8)** __________ loves burgers, too? (33) __________

106 !! Word formation: Different Lifestyles, Different Ways of Travelling

You are going to read a text about different forms of travelling. Some words are missing from the text. Use the words in brackets to complete each gap (1–14) in the text. Write your answers in the spaces provided at the end of the text. The first one (0) has been done for you.

Different Lifestyles, Different Ways of Travelling

Nowadays modern travelling can be **(0)** ____ **(definition)** as follows: people leave their homes in order to spend some days or weeks at a comfortable **(1)** ____ **(accommodate)** with hardly any physical and mental exercise and lots of delicious food. Modern travel is all about entertainment, amusement and having fun. It is **(2)** ____ **(devotion)** to personal enrichment, pleasure and relaxation. And it is meant to satisfy people, make them come home again happy, refreshed and **(3)** ____ **(energy)**. Modern tourism does not promise transformation, spiritual or emotional enlargement or change. On the contrary, it offers the possibility to leave home and return after some time without any significant change or challenge. Flights, hotels, sightseeing or boat tours and even hired cars are mostly booked in advance. And once people arrive at their holiday destination, they lie back in their deckchairs and **(4)** ____ **(enjoyment)** themselves and their holiday. A holiday for which they have worked hard enough because travelling has turned into an extremely costly and expensive business, which nowadays only people who make good money can afford. Thus modern tourism has clearly turned into something reserved for the privileged and wealthy.

What people often forget, however, is the fact that travelling has also got a second meaning. A meaning that is much more significant and that goes back to the origin of **(5)** ____ **(human)**. In the Bible, for example, the human journey begins with an expulsion. God's chosen people – Adam and Eve – are **(6)** ____ **(condemnation)** to wander and to leave paradise. Ever since then individuals have been wandering around, have moved from one place to another, from one country to another, to either stay there or to go on wandering. And indeed, this rearrangement – temporary as well as permanent – is nowadays as essential and fundamental to modern life as the Internet, global trade or any other sociological development. Today life is characterized by extreme **(7)** ____ **(immobile)**, which, in the widest sense, has also led to migration. Leaving one country or continent in order to move to another no longer causes any difficulties, problems or real challenges. And if we want to, we might think of a migrant as a traveller without a return ticket.

Certainly, the reasons for travelling have changed as well. While in ancient times journeys were marked by mythical and religious significance, people today no longer pack their bags in order to find oracles or certain Gods. What has **(8)** ____ **(remnant)**, though, is the idea of pilgrimage and the idea of taking one's most important and necessary possessions and belongings and to simply start walking – either for just some days or even for some months, depending on how much time you can and want to invest. This type of travelling is the journey to oneself and the way to one's soul and spirit. It is a journey one has to be ready for because while it is often tiring and exhausting – mostly in an emotional way – it is a journey full of surprises about oneself and about one's personality. When asked about their motivation, pilgrims often say that the best thing about a pilgrimage is the fact that you do not always know where you are, what to expect, how to communicate, where to sleep and sometimes even what to eat. It is an adventure that often makes people **(9)** ____ **(anxiety)**, uneasy or even afraid because things are *not* planned and *not* organised.

So, what finally distinguishes meaningful, fruitful travel from mere tourism? What turns travel into a quest rather than pre-arranged escapism? Of course, people's opinions differ when it comes to answering these questions. There is no doubt, though, that when we travel we are asking for **(10)** ______ **(hospitable)**. We get in touch with other people, sometimes we are dependent on them and we might even end up being helpless. There is, of course, great vulnerability in this, which also requires considerable **(11)** ______ **(strong)**. Of course it is much easier to just pack a suitcase, board an airplane and spend a fortnight on the beaches of Bali with your partner. But there won't be much getting in touch with other people, other cultures, other traditions, other points of view and other habits. There won't be much getting in touch with your inner self, your problems, sorrows, worries and fears. Travel is always a search for meaning as well, not only in our own lives but also in the lives of others.

Therefore, the greatest difference between travel and tourism could be that tourism is safe, controlled and predetermined. No doubt, this is comfortable and easy. Travel, in contrast, is about the **(12)** ______ **(expectation)**, the surprising, about giving oneself over to disorientation and maybe even chaos. And if this sounds tiring, then it certainly is. But not **(13)** ______ **(necessity)** in a physical way. Travel does not automatically mean pain or excessive strain. It does not automatically mean hurting feet and blisters. It does not have to be an extreme sport. It means being ready to be oneself again, to be clumsy, inexperienced and maybe even a bit lonely. It means wandering back towards oneself at whatever pace and speed. And this is the paradox: pilgrims set out on adventures to gain deeper access to themselves.

In the end it is not the question whether one type of travelling is better than the other. We simply have two extremes, and obviously both forms have their fans and supporters. It is not necessary, either, to choose between them because genuine travel and tourism do not **(14)** ______ **(competition)** with each other. They are just different options for all the different people and individuals that our world is made up of.

0. *defined*

1. ______________________

2. ______________________

3. ______________________

4. ______________________

5. ______________________

6. ______________________

7. ______________________

8. ______________________

9. ______________________

10. ______________________

11. ______________________

12. ______________________

13. ______________________

14. ______________________

107 ! Follow-up task: Connect the ideas with a relative pronoun (who/which/that) to form sentences. Mind commas.

EXAMPLE only individuals – make good money – can afford a holiday
Only individuals who make good money can afford a holiday.

1. travelling – something – goes back – to the beginnings of humanity

2. Adam and Eve – condemned – leave paradise – forced to wander around

3. people – move – from one country to another – called migrants

4. rearrangements – essential for modern life – omnipresent

5. pilgrims – people – want to find their inner peace

6. pilgrims meet other individuals – never met before *(mind the tense!)*

108 !! Translate, using who or which.

EXAMPLE Ich kann nicht sagen, welche Art des Reisens besser ist.
I can't say which type of travelling is better.

1. Kennst du jemanden, der eine Pilgerreise gemacht hat?

2. Während meiner Pilgerreisen hoffe ich immer darauf, Menschen zu treffen, die mir helfen.

109 !! Word formation: Climate Change

You are going to read a text about climate change. Some words are missing. Use the words in brackets to complete each gap (1–8) in the text. Write your answers in the spaces provided at the end of the text. The first one (0) has been done for you.

New Study Forces Critical Scientists to Change their Minds

Every child knows it – we produce too much waste, **(0)** .... **(emission)** too much CO_2, and constantly pollute planet Earth. That's why so many people talk about saving the environment, go on protest marches and try to protect what has not yet been ruined by mankind. The Earth's surface has warmed **(1)** .... **(consideration)** over the past 250 years, and crucial consequences **(2)** .... **(relation)** to this process can already be observed. Take the glaciers as an example. The ice layers of the glaciers constantly diminish and the glaciers shrink, which poses a dangerous threat to wildlife and the ecological balance. Humans are almost **(3)** .... **(entire)** the cause for this rise in temperature, at least according to a number of scientific studies carried out to address the concerns of sceptics about whether human **(4)** .... **(induction)** global warming really exists or not.

However, opinions among experts will always differ, and when it comes to the topic of climate change, this is no exception. Some **(5)** .... **(scientific)**, for instance, doubt the results of the studies just mentioned, claiming that they were not wide-reaching enough and therefore lack a certain **(6)** .... **(valid)**. They do not believe that the carbon dioxide in the Earth's atmosphere, measured from atmospheric samples and air trapped in polar ice, actually **(7)** .... **(proof)** that global warming is caused by human greenhouse gases. So, who is right and who are we to believe? The major problem is that whenever scientists come up with new results, they face **(8)** .... **(hostile)** when expressing alternative or controversial views.

Thus, when we consider all this scientific "in-fighting", it's hardly possible for us to make up our minds. People like you and me do not understand enough about these matters and their possible interpretations. The only thing we understand is that temperatures do seem to rise and that summers as well as winters seem to get warmer.

0. *emit*
1. ....
2. ....
3. ....
4. ....
5. ....
6. ....
7. ....
8. ....

REPORTED OR INDIRECT SPEECH – INDIREKTE REDE

A Grundsätzliches zur indirekten Rede

- Wenn wir jemand mitteilen möchten, was jemand anderer gesagt hat, verwendet man die „indirekte Rede". Sie umfasst **Aussagen, Fragen, Bitten** und **Verbote**.
- Zur Einleitung der indirekten Rede dient eine Reihe von Verben, die ***reporting verbs***. Die häufigsten sind:

reporting verbs				
answer	explain	mention	say	want to know
ask	inform	remember	tell	wonder
complain	know	report	think	write

B *the indirect command* – Der indirekte Befehl

- Der indirekte Befehl umfasst vom Inhalt her **Befehle, Aufforderungen, Bitten** und **Verbote**.
- Die häufigsten ***reporting verbs*** für den indirekten Befehl sind:

  tell bei Befehlen, Aufforderungen und Verboten
  ask bei Bitten und höflichen Aufforderungen

- Den indirekten Befehl bildet man mit dem **Infinitiv (Nennform, *to-form, base form*)**. (Bei einer anderen Art des indirekten Befehls wird aus dem direkten Befehl eine indirekte Aussage mit ***should/should not***.)

- **Aufforderung:**
  *Ms Gibson said, "**Read** chapters 2 and 3!"*
  *Ms Gibson **told** us **to read** chapers 2 and 3.*
  *(Ms Gibson said we **should read** chapters 2 and 3.)*

- **Befehl:**
  *The policeman said, "**Get** out of the car!"*
  *The policeman **told** me **to get** out of the car.*
  *(The policeman said I **should get** out of the car.)*

- **Bitte, höfliche Aufforderung:**
  *Travis said, "Please **come** in and **sit** down!"*
  *Travis **asked** us **to come** in and **sit** down.*
  *(Travis said we **should come** in and **sit** down.)*

- **Verbot:**
  *Jackie said, "**Don't open** the door!"*
  *Jackie **told** us **not to open** the door.*
  *(Jackie said we **shouldn't open** the door.)*
  *Jackie said, "Don't open the door, **please**!"*
  *Jackie **asked** us **not to open** the door.*

110 Put the commands into reported speech. Write two versions.

EXAMPLE The English teacher said, "Do numbers two and three!"
The English teacher told us to do numbers two and three.
The English teacher said we should do numbers two and three.

1. The policeman said to the young woman, "Show me your driving licence!"

2. Mummy told little Benjamin, "Don't talk to strangers!"

3. Dad told Joshua, "Be home before midnight!"

4. Gabriel said, "Mark, don't go out with Veronica!"

111 ! Match the sentence halves. Write the letters into the boxes.

1.	Lisa tells her best friend Tina	**A**	his blue trainers are.
2.	Dad tells Frederick	**B**	to have my pink scarf.
3.	Ina reminds Luis not to forget	**C**	was very nice last week.
4.	Pia informs me that she wants	**D**	an A on the last French test.
5.	Neill wonders where	**E**	that they have a test today.
6.	Leo remembers that he must	**F**	pupils not to use dictionaries.
7.	Sophia says that she has got	**G**	stay in bed all week.
8.	Paul said that we should	**H**	that she is in love with Nick.
9.	The children remind the teacher	**I**	doesn't need any help.
10.	The English teacher tells the	**J**	in bed until I feel better.
11.	Mrs Watson insists that she	**K**	go to the dentist.
12.	Nora reports that the weather	**L**	if this is the last sentence.
13.	The doctor orders me to stay	**M**	to be home in time.
14.	I reply that I will certainly	**N**	be quiet.
15.	I want to know from you	**O**	to do the shopping.

1	2	3	4	5	6	7	8	9	10	11	12	13	14	15
H														

C ! *change of tenses* – Verschiebung der Zeitstufen

Meistens erzählen wir zu einem späteren Zeitpunkt weiter, was jemand zu uns gesagt hat. Das ***reporting verb*** steht daher **in *past tense***, und in der Folge verschieben sich auch die Zeiten der direkten Rede nach ganz bestimmten Regeln. Das gilt für Aussagen und Fragen. (Wenn das *reporting verb* in *present tense, present perfect tense oder future tense* steht, gibt es keine Verschiebung der Zeitstufen!)

direct speech *Joe said, "…"*	***reported speech*** *Joe said (that) …*
present tense *"I **like** tea."* *"The sun **is shining**."*	***past tense*** *… he **liked** tea.* *… the sun **was shining**.*
past tense *"Lots of people **were** there."* *"We **were talking** about you."*	***past perfect tense*** *… lots of people **had been** there.* *… they **had been talking** about me.* (oder: *… they **were talking** about me.*)
present perfect tense *"It **has stopped** raining."* *"Jill **has been crying** since the morning."*	***past perfect tense*** *… it **had stopped** raining.* *… Jill **had been crying** since the morning.*
will *"They **will come** again soon."*	***would*** *… they **would come** again soon.*
am/is/are going to *"We**'re going to** win."*	***was/were going to*** *… they **were going to** win.*
can – may *"Things **can** only get better."* *"It **may** be dangerous."*	***could – might*** *… things **could** only get better.* *… it **might** be dangerous.*
must ***must not*** *„We **must** leave at once."* *"I **mustn't** be late again."*	***must / had to*** ***must not*** *… they **must** leave at once.* *… they **had to** leave at once.* *… he **mustn't** be late again.*

Einige Verben verändern sich nicht beim Übergang von direkter zu indirekter Rede:

- ***could – would – should – might – ought to – used to***
- **alle** Verben in ***past perfect tense***

D *change of adverbials* – Verschiebungen bei Orts- und Zeitangaben

Orts- und Zeitangaben verändern sich sinngemäß, wenn „Hier“ nicht mehr „Hier“ ist und „Gestern“ nicht mehr „Gestern“.

Auch hier geht man nach einem Schema vor:

direct	*reported*	*direct*	*reported*
this	***that***	*(two days) ago*	*(two days)* ***before***
these	***those***	*last (week)*	*(the week)* ***before*** ***the previous*** *(week)*
yesterday	***the day before*** ***the previous day***	*next (week)*	*(the week)* ***after*** ***the following*** *(week)*
today	***that day***	*here*	***there***
tomorrow	***the day after*** ***the next/following day***	*now*	**fällt weg**, oder … ***then*** **–** ***at that time***

E *indirect questions* – Indirekte Fragen

- Die Bildung der indirekten Frage hängt davon ab, ob es sich um eine **Entscheidungsfrage oder** eine **Ergänzungsfrage** handelt.

Entscheidungsfrage ***(yes or no?)***	
	Sarah asked me …
*“**Is** Mike at home?”*	*… **if/whether** Mike **was** at home.*
*“**Will** you **help** me?”*	*… **if/whether** we **would help** her.*
*“**Do** the Coopers **live** here?”*	*… **if/whether** the Coopers **lived** there.*
*“**Did** you come by bus?”*	*… **if/whether** I **had come** by bus.*
	ob **=** ***if*** **oder** ***whether***

Ergänzungsfrage ***(Who? Where? When? How? …)***	
	Jack wanted to know …
*“**Where do** you **live**?”*	*… **where** we **lived**.*
*“**How can** I help you?”*	*… **how** he **could** help me.*
*“**When will** Ron **be** back again?”*	*… **when** Ron **would be** back again.*
*“**Why haven’t** you **called** us?”*	*… **why** I **hadn’t called** them.*
	Fragewort wird weiterverwendet

- **Indirekte Fragen sind in Wahrheit Aussagen.**
  Es gibt daher …
  – keine Anführungszeichen;
  – kein Fragezeichen;
  – die „normale“ Wortfolge *(word order)*: **S – P – O.**

112 ! Put the following statements into reported speech.

EXAMPLE Samantha told Linda, "I have already seen the new TV series that started last week."
Samantha told Linda that she had already seen the new TV series that had started the week before.

1. Nicolas said to Tobi, "I think we haven't seen each other since the graduation party six weeks ago."

2. Susanna informed her mum, "I am going to paint my room black next summer holidays."

3. Jackie complained, "My boyfriend never brings me flowers and doesn't care about my feelings!"

4. Irina remembered happily, "I was writing a message to Matthias when he suddenly phoned me!"

5. Benjamin remarked angrily, "If I had studied more, I would have got better grades."

6. Vanessa thought, "I will be fitter if I exercise more from now on."

113 ! **Read about Thomas and put his questions into reported speech.**

Hi, I'm Thomas and I am 16 years old. I attend Crosswill High School in Cornwall and I have to confess that I worry about a lot of things! First, I worry about girls, because I'm not very popular with them ☹. Then, of course, I worry about my grades because while I'm brilliant in English, I'm rubbish at maths. Finally, I worry about my parents, because they constantly get on my nerves. For sure, there is much more to worry about as you will find out in the following questions …

EXAMPLE Thomas asked himself, "Will I ever find a nice and pretty girlfriend?"
Thomas asked himself *if he would ever find a nice and pretty girlfriend.*

1. Thomas asked himself, "Where and when can I meet nice girls?"

   Thomas asked himself ……………………………………

   ……………………………………

2. Thomas asked himself, "How might I get better at maths?"

   Thomas asked himself ……………………………………

   ……………………………………

3. Thomas asked himself, "What can I do to stop my parents getting on my nerves?"

   Thomas asked himself ……………………………………

   ……………………………………

4. Thomas asked himself, "Why are all my friends allowed to stay out longer?"

   Thomas asked himself ……………………………………

   ……………………………………

5. Thomas asked himself, "What ways are there to get more pocket money?"

   Thomas asked himself ……………………………………

   ……………………………………

6. Thomas asked himself, "Is it really necessary to learn so much about trigonometry?"

   Thomas asked himself ……………………………………

   ……………………………………

114 !! Read the dialogue and put it into reported speech.

Natalie: Hi Greg, it's nice to see you again! I haven't seen you for quite a while!
Greg: Yes, that's true. I was on holiday with my family.
Natalie: Really? Where were you? How long did you stay?
Greg: I was in India for three weeks. It was a birthday present.
Natalie: Did you know about this special surprise before?
Greg: No, I didn't, so I was really surprised when I opened the envelope and found the flight tickets to New Delhi.
Natalie: I can imagine! You must tell me all about it!
Greg: I will, Natalie! Next time we meet, I'll bring along my iPad to show you some pictures.
Natalie: Yes, please! Looking forward to seeing you again, Greg! Bye!
Greg: Bye Natalie, and have a nice day!

EXAMPLE Natalie said hi to Greg, adding that ***it was nice to see him again because she hadn't seen him for quite a while.***

Greg replied that that .... and

explained that ....

Natalie was amazed and wanted to know ....

....

Greg informed her that ....

....

Natalie asked ....

Greg said no, he ....

....

....

Natalie confirmed that ....

and said that Greg ....

Greg said .... and told her that ....

....

Natalie agreed and mentioned that ....

....

When Natalie had said goodbye, Greg wished her a nice day.

115 !! Multiple choice: Alaska

You are going to read an interview with Joshua Watson, an expert on planning and carrying out expeditions to Alaska. Some words are missing from the text. Choose the correct answer (A, B or C) for each gap (1–8). Then write your answers in the space provided. The first one (0) has been done for you.

Reporter: Hi Joshua, it is nice to have you here and thanks for doing the interview with us!
Joshua: **(0)** ____ I'm always happy when people are interested in what I do!
Reporter: Joshua, how long have you been organising expeditions to Alaska?
Joshua: Well, I've been doing this for about eighteen years now. I first joined an Alaska expedition when I **(1)** ____ university and I was absolutely amazed and fascinated. I simply got hooked. So I quickly finished my studies, founded my own adventure and outdoor company, and it soon became a success. I love the business I'm working in and I'd never do anything else. Never!
Reporter: Wonderful! But what exactly fascinates you about Alaska?
Joshua: First of all, it's the **(2)** ____ landscape, the high snowy mountains and all the glaciers (= *Gletscher*). The weather is usually very cold and rough and often storms roll through the Alaska Range. This is when the **(3)** ____ temperatures feel even more freezing. I think the lowest temperature measured was -80°F.
Reporter: Wow, that's unbelievable! Isn't a place like Alaska very dangerous then?
Joshua: Of course it is! But if you know what you are doing and **(4)** ____ safety precautions, travelling there is no more dangerous than travelling to any other mountain area. What you **(5)** ____ take into consideration, however, is the weather and the high annual snowfall, the crevasses (= *Gletscherspalten*) and the amount of daylight.
Reporter: The amount of daylight? What do you mean?
Joshua: Well, the daylight hours vary depending on when you travel there. While it never **(6)** ____ dark in June and July, you only have six hours of daylight or less in December and January. This is due to the extreme northern latitude (= *Breitengrad*).
Reporter: Are there also any dangerous animals in Alaska?
Joshua: Certainly, yes! You find many brown bears and grizzlies, but then again, if you know how to behave, you **(7)** ____ any serious problems.
Reporter: Tell me, Joshua, isn't America's highest mountain in Alaska, too?
Joshua: Yes, it's called Denali, or Mount McKinley. Its peak is 6194 meters high and it's certainly one of the world's greatest challenges. After all, it was first climbed only in 1913.
Reporter: Many thanks for this **(8)** ____ and informative interview, Joshua!

0	A	Your welcome!	B	*You're welcome!*	C	Please!
1	A	was at	B	visited	C	went to
2	A	good	B	amazing	C	urban
3	A	low	B	moderate	C	high
4	A	plan	B	make	C	take
5	A	need	B	mustn't	C	must
6	A	gets	B	is	C	becomes
7	A	won't have	B	wouldn't have	C	wouldn't get
8	A	interresting	B	interesting	C	interessting

0	1	2	3	4	5	6	7	8
B								

116 !! Follow-up task: Put the interview's content into reported speech.

EXAMPLE I'm always happy when people are interested in what I do!
Joshua said *he was always happy when people were interested in what he did.*

1. How long have you been organising expeditions to Alaska, Joshua?

   The reporter wanted to know ……………………………………………………………

   ……………………………………………………………………………………………

2. I've been doing them for about eight years now.

   Joshua replied that ……………………………………………………………………

   ……………………………………………………………………………………………

3. What exactly is so fascinating about Alaska for you?

   The reporter wondered ………………………………………………………………

   ……………………………………………………………………………………………

4. I think the lowest temperature they measured was -80°F.

   Joshua thought that ……………………………………………………………………

   ……………………………………………………………………………………………

5. Are there also dangerous animals in Alaska?

   The reporter enquired …………………………………………………………………

   ……………………………………………………………………………………………

6. Of course there are! But if you know how to behave, you won't have any serious problems.

   Joshua replied that ……………………………………………………………………

   ……………………………………………………………………………………………

   ……………………………………………………………………………………………

7. What is the highest mountain in Alaska?

   Finally the reporter asked ……………………………………………………………

   ……………………………………………………………………………………………

117 !! Multiple choice: The Royal Baby

You are going to read a text about the English royal offspring. Some words are missing from the text. Choose the correct answer (A, B, C or D) for each gap (1–10). Then write your answers in the space provided. The first one (0) has been done for you.

William and Kate's Baby Prince Presented

On July 22nd, 2013, the entire British nation broke out in cheers to welcome William and Kate's baby, who will be known as Prince George Alexander Louis of Cambridge. Many Brits confirmed that they **(0)** ______ eagerly for this moment to happen.

Weeks before the official birth date of the little prince, journalists and reporters had already positioned themselves outside St Mary's Hospital in West London, making sure they would get the first glimpse of the newborn baby. Some even said that taking the first picture **(1)** ______ their careers significantly and could lead to enormous success and wealth. In the meantime, speculation on the baby's name ran high. Bookmakers, for example, reported that numbers of incoming bets **(2)** ______, favouring the names George and James for boys. Names like Edward and Charles, however, were considered unlikely. The media also announced that possible names for girls **(3)** ______ Charlotte and Alexandra.

It was announced by the Royal Press Agency that Kate's delivery **(4)** ______ short and unproblematic, and indeed she left the hospital's private Lindo Wing one day later. Walking out, she was cheered by staff and well-wishers, and while cradling her son lovingly she said that she **(5)** ______ happier in her life. The proud father, William, jokingly commented that the baby luckily **(6)** ______ the mother's looks and not his. When speaking to reporters later on, the couple said that the birth experience **(7)** ______ very emotional. Then William drove his new family home to Kensington Palace. Of course, little George is going to have a nanny. It has been said that Anna Fresolone, the former Queen's maid, **(8)** ______ in charge of the baby.

Not surprisingly, the birth of the royal baby has boosted sales figures of souvenirs enormously, and hundreds of mugs and cups with pictures of little George **(9)** ______ already. Speculation and gossip on Kate's looks are equally high. While some magazines wrote that she had a personal trainer and **(10)** ______ to lose her excess baby weight as soon as possible, other media highly criticised this step, considering it as unhealthy and unnatural. Either way, the British Nation is totally in love with their young Royal Family and wants nothing but the best for Little George's future.

0	A	had waited	B	were waiting	C	waited	D	*had been waiting*
1	A	will push	B	would push	C	pushes	D	will have pushed
2	A	would soar	B	have soared	C	soared	D	had soared
3	A	might be	B	may be	C	are	D	might have been
4	A	has been	B	had been	C	was	D	had been having
5	A	was never	B	was never been	C	is never	D	had never been
6	A	will have	B	has	C	had	D	has had
7	A	is	B	was	C	has been	D	had been
8	A	was going to be	B	would be	C	will be	D	is going to be
9	A	have been sold	B	would be sold	C	are sold	D	had been sold
10	A	had tried	B	would try	C	has tried	D	is going to try

0	1	2	3	4	5	6	7	8	9	10
D										

TENSES: PRESENT TENSE – GEGENWART

A Formen von *present tense*

present simple		***present progressive***		
active				
I – you – we – they	***ask***	*I*	***am***	***asking***
he – she – it	***asks***	*he – she – it*	***is***	***asking***
		we – you – they	***are***	***asking***
wie Nennform (***infinitive***) – außer 3. Person Einzahl (***infinitive + s/es***)		Bildung mit ***am/is/are* + “*ing-form*”**		
passive				
am/is/are asked		***am/is/are being asked***		

Mehr Informationen ab Seite 88.

B Anwendung von *present simple* und *present progressive*

	present simple	
a	Tatsachen unveränderliche Zustände	*The moon* ***circles*** *the Earth every 28 days.* *Polar bears* ***live*** *in the Arctic.*
b	regelmäßig oder immer wieder stattfindende Handlungen (*always, often, never, usually …*)	*It often* ***rains*** *in the mountains.* *My parents never* ***forget*** *a promise.*
c	zeitlich genau festgelegte zukünftige Ereignisse	*Joe's bus* ***arrives*** *in 20 minutes.* *When* ***does*** *the party* ***begin****?*
	present progressive	
d	Handlungen, die im Augenblick des Sprechens („jetzt gerade“) stattfinden oder noch nicht beendet sind	*I* ***am preparing*** *for a test.* *What* ***are*** *you* ***doing*** *here?* *Be quiet! The baby* ***is sleeping****.*
e	Ausnahmen oder Handlungen, die von der „Norm“ abweichen	*Mum usually takes the bus to work, but today she* ***is driving****.* *I like movies, but I****'m*** *not* ***going*** *tonight.*
f	Ereignisse in der nahen Zukunft (mit Zeitangabe)	*We* ***are meeting*** *some friends after school.* *Mike* ***is*** *not* ***coming*** *on Saturday.*
g	mit *always*, um Ärger oder Verstimmung auszudrücken	*Harry* ***is always sitting*** *on my chair.* *I****'m always losing*** *against you!*

118 Present tense simple or progressive?

1. Oh, look outside – it **is raining** *(rain)* heavily and the wind .... *(blow)*. I really .... *(not know)* what to do on a day like this!
2. Usually Moira .... *(check)* her emails every day, but today she .... *(not check)* them because her laptop has broken down. Now she .... *(be)* desperate.
3. My mum .... *(call)* me every day and I really .... *(think)* that this is extremely annoying. But if I .... *(tell)* her to stop calling me, she just gets angry.
4. Alex, tell me, why .... *(you/wear)* this silly brown sports cap? It really .... *(look)* stupid on you.
5. Please be quiet. Little Benny .... *(sleep)* and I .... *(not want)* him to wake up.
6. Why .... *(Tina / not tell)* me the truth? I think I have a right to know why she .... *(behave)* so strangely these days.

119 Find the correct questions to the given answers.

EXAMPLE ***Have you got a pet? (Do you have a pet?)***
Yes, I have! It's a dog and his name is *Buddy*.

1. ....?

   Yes, he is. Can't you hear him snoring?

2. ....?

   Well, it's fine. There is sunshine and it's quite warm.

3. ....?

   Yes, he has. Her name's Lia, she's very pretty, and Bob's in love with her.

4. ....?

   No, I'm not. I've already done the one for English at school.

TENSES: PAST TENSE – MITVERGANGENHEIT/IMPERFEKT

A Formen von *past tense*

past simple		*past progressive*
active		
regular verbs	***irregular verbs***	kein Unterschied zwischen *regular* und *irregular*
*wash**ed***	***brought***	***was** wash**ing** / **were** bring**ing***
*rul**ed***	***flew***	***was** rul**ing** / **were** fly**ing***
*collect**ed***	***did***	***was** collect**ing** / **were** do**ing***
infinitive + (e)d	***past form/2nd form***	***was/were + ing-form***
passive		
was/were washed		***was/were being washed***
was/were brought		***was/were being brought***

Mehr Informationen ab Seite 88.

B Anwendung von *past simple* und *past progressive*

	past simple	
a	für Ereignisse aus der Vergangenheit, die abgeschlossen und vorbei sind	*Elizabeth I **ruled** England in the 16th century. The colonists **brought** plants and animals from Europe with them.*
b	zum Erzählen von Geschichten; *past simple* ist die „Erzählzeit"	*A rich man's wife **became** sick, and when she **felt** that her end **was** near, she **called** for her only daughter and **said** …*
	past progressive	
c	für Handlungen, die zu einem vergangenen Zeitpunkt gerade im Ablaufen waren	*Yesterday at this time, I **was flying** over the Atlantic Ocean. What **were** you **doing** at 5 p.m. last Friday?*
d	für zwei oder mehrere parallel ablaufende vergangene Handlungen; meist durch *while* verbunden	***While** I **was watching** TV last night, my upstairs neighbours **were having** a fight again.*
e	kurze Handlung (*past simple*) „unterbricht" längere Handlung (*past progressive*); meist durch *when* verbunden	***When** the fire **broke** out, most people **were sleeping**.*

120 ! Past tense simple or progressive? Complete the dialogue.

Luis: Hi Bart, I haven't seen you for quite a while! Are you alright?

Bart: Of course I am. I **was** *(be)* in Spain for half a year and I have just returned.

Luis: In Spain! Wow, that sounds cool! Where exactly ________________ *(you/be)*?

Bart: I was in Alicante, that's a town directly on the Costa Blanca. I ________________ *(get)* there March and I ________________ *(return)* only last Thursday.

Luis: Can you tell me more about it? What ________________ *(you/do)* there for such a long time?

Bart: Actually I ________________ *(go)* there to earn some money and to get to know another culture and lifestyle. I ________________ *(want)* to work in a restaurant but I ________________ *(have)* problems with my boss and so I ________________ *(stop)* working there after a few weeks.

Luis: That sounds exciting but stressful! So what ________________ *(you/do)*?

Bart: I ________________ *(think)* about flying back home when I ________________ *(meet)* a guy who was planning to open his own beach bar. We ________________ *(talk)* about his project for ages, and then he suddenly ________________ *(ask)* me if I wanted to join him. At first I wasn't sure and ________________ *(not know)* what to do, but then I simply ________________ *(agree)*.

Luis: So how does the story go on?

Bart: Well, we ________________ *(buy)* an abandoned café, adapted it a bit, ________________ *(invest)* some money and ________________ *(open)* our beach bar, which we ________________ *(call)* *El Baile*.

Luis: But why are you here now and not in Spain?

Bart: I ________________ *(decide)* to move to Spain for good, so I'm just here to say goodbye to my friends, and then I'm off again.

121 ! Complete the sentence halves.

1.	My mobile rang while my teacher	7.	listening to music on my iPhone.
2.	During our last French test, Linda		I had breakfast. Later I left home.
3.	At first I took a shower and then		her about our delay?
4.	Were you really trying to impress		her eyeliner fell into the toilet.
5.	Did you call Barbara to inform		Latin homework, were you?
6.	Robin, you weren't doing your		was trying to explain the tenses.
7.	Nick was watching TV while I was		red roses like I said?
8.	Mia was putting on make-up when		was copying from her neighbour.
9.	Paul, did you buy the bunch of		me with this silly performance?

122 Circle the correct option.

1. My dog Gini *ran* / *was running* through the woods while I *tried* / *was trying* to find her again. Unfortunately it *took* / *was taking* me quite a while.
2. What *did you do* / *were you doing* yesterday at half past five p.m.?
3. I *watered* / *was watering* the flowers when it *started* / *was starting* to rain.
4. *Did she know* / *Was she knowing* that Charles was married?
5. *Didn't Adele give* / *Wasn't Adele giving* an interview when she broke down?
6. Where *did you meet* / *were you meeting* the rest of the group?

123 !! Translate the sentences with past simple.

EXAMPLE Ich versuchte dich anzurufen, als die Lichter ausgingen.
I was trying to phone you when the lights went out.

1. Wie lange hast du gestern auf mich gewartet?

2. Wo warst du Sonntag Nachmittag?

3. She sah mich traurig an, dann drehte sich sich um und ging weg.

4. Hast du die Französisch-Hausübung abgeschrieben?

124 **!** **Read the fairy tale and fill in the correct tense: present (simple/progressive) or past (simple/progressive).**

Once upon a time there was a king who **lived** (*live*) in a country far away. His name was King Philipp and he had a beautiful daughter called Sophia.

One day King Philipp .... (*go*) to Sophia's room and sat down on a chair in front of the big window. He .... (*look*) at his daughter while she .... (*brush*) her long blond hair. "Daughter, I need to talk to you", he finally said after a few minutes. Sophia put away her hairbrush at once and looked straight at her father. "What is it you want to talk about?", she replied. "Your mother and I, we have agreed that it is time for you to marry. We have already thought about a couple of possible husbands and we want you to meet them. Then we .... (*expect*) you to decide who you want to marry and .... (*spend*) the rest of your life with."

As Sophia was a very obedient daughter, she did what her parents .... (*expect*) of her. She .... (*meet*) all the different men and got to know them better. But unfortunately she liked none of them. Most were dull and boring or simply stupid. But then, very unexpectedly, two men appeared who were different compared with all the others. One was called Leo, and he was very handsome and charming. Sophia was fascinated and enjoyed every minute she spent with him. The other man, whose name was Alex, was not that good-looking, but he was gentle and caring and Sophia liked that a lot, too.

After a few weeks King Philipp came to his daughter's room again. "Now tell me, Daughter, who .... (*you/want*) to marry?" Sophia was desperate because she .... (*not know*) what to say. Who should she marry – Leo or Alex? Each of them had something special and desirable, and if she .... (*choose*) the one, she would definitely miss the other. "Father, I .... (*not know*) because I love both of them", she finally said, looking very sad. King Phillipp .... (*look*) at his daughter and then replied, "This night a fairy will appear in your dreams and she will tell you what to do. Listen to her and promise me to follow her advice."

Sophia .... (*do*) as she was told, and really, a golden-haired fairy appeared in her dream that night. She said, "When all the snow has melted, you will find a rosebush growing in your garden. Wait for its first flowers. If they are red, marry Alex. If they are white, marry Leo." Then the fairy disappeared again and Sophia had a peaceful and quiet sleep.

Soon the days were getting warmer again, all the snow .... (*melt*) and a wonderful rosebush really began to grow. Sophia was very excited and looked at it every day. She .... (*can*) hardly wait for it to blossom. And then, on a sunny spring day, her patience was rewarded: there was a beautiful, shiny, velvety rose and its colour was red! Quickly, Sophia .... (*run*) back into the palace and to the king's room. "Father, it's Alex I want to be together with. Now I .... (*know*) for sure!" She smiled happily.

That summer King Philipp organised a wonderful wedding and .... (*invite*) hundreds of people. Sophia and Alex, however, lived happily ever after.

TENSES: PRESENT PERFECT TENSE – VERGANGENHEIT, PERFEKT

A Formen von *present perfect tense*

present perfect simple		*present perfect progressive*	
active			
I – you – we – they	***have (not) asked***	*I – you – we – they*	***have been asking****
he – she – it	***has (not) asked***	*he – she – it*	***has been asking****
have/has (not) + 3rd form		***have/has been + ing-form****	
passive			
have/has (not) been asked		–	

* Kommt in der Verneinung nicht vor

B ! Anwendung von *present perfect simple*

- *Present perfect simple* sieht ähnlich aus wie die deutsche Vergangenheit, aber in der Anwendung gibt es große Unterschiede.
- Sie wird für Handlungen verwendet, die (meist kurz) vor dem **„Hier und Jetzt“** geschehen sind und deren Auswirkungen oder Folgen auf das „Hier und Jetzt“ noch spürbar sind. Dabei ist es unwichtig, wann die Dinge geschehen sind; wichtig ist, dass oder ob sie geschehen sind und sich daher auf das „Hier und Jetzt“ auswirken.

*The lights **have gone** out.* → Egal wann; jetzt ist es dunkel.
*Oliver **hasn't answered** my e-mail.* → Ich weiß daher nicht, ob er kommt.
***Have** you **seen** my glasses?* → Kannst du mir daher sagen, wo sie sind?

- Bestimmte Wörter lassen den Bezug zum „Hier und Jetzt“ erkennen:

just	soeben, gerade	***today, all day***	heute, den ganzen Tag
already	schon, bereits	***this (week …)***	diese (Woche …)
ever?	schon (einmal)?	***in the last few (hours, days …)***	in den letzten paar (Stunden, Tagen …)
never	nie, noch nie		
so far	bis jetzt	***yet?***	schon? bereits?
recently, lately	vor kurzem	***not yet***	noch nicht

*I'**ve just got** a message from Tony. Everything's okay.*
*I'm sorry, Emily isn't here. She'**s left** for school **already**.*
***Has** anyone **ever seen** a better movie than Hitchcock's "Psycho"?*
*Our team **has never won** a championship title.*
*Richard **has spent** only 35 € **so far**. That's not much.*
*We'**ve read** some good books **recently**. (… **lately**.)*
*It **hasn't rained** here **all day** / **this week** / **in the last few days** / …*
***Have** you **done** your homework **yet**? – I **haven't** even **started yet**!*

125 Form present perfect simple sentences.

EXAMPLE star / never / a / I / have / met
I have never met a star.

1. eaten / too / cake / she / much / has

2. ever / a / have / lie? / you / told

3. yet / we / bill / not / the / have / paid

4. Michelle / love / has / ever / in / ever / fallen / before?

126 ! Transform the nouns (in brackets) into verbs, then put them into present perfect simple. The first one has been done for you.

EXAMPLE Carol **has** never **known** (*knowledge*) a lot about mathematics.

1. Litte Benny ________ (*invitation*) all his friends to the party.
2. My parents ________ (*sale*) our house. Now we live in a flat.
3. My brother ________ (*break up*) with his girlfriend Melissa.
4. ________ (*you/already/download*) the DJ Antoine song?
5. I ________ (*not/obedience*) my dad, so now I'm grounded.
6. The train from Belfast ________ (*already/arrival*).
7. ________ the airplane ________ (*take-off*) yet?
8. Angelina and Frank ________ (*separation*) recently.
9. Oh no! Larry ________ (*just/ruin*) my new mobile!
10. ________ (*you/ever/invention*) something useful?
11. ________ (*Jim/ever/building*) a house?
12. Can you tell me if the train ________ (*already/departure*)?
13. Cindy ________ (*not/usage*) the Internet for five days.
14. I ________ (*never/painting*) a portrait so far.
15. I think I ________ (*completion*) this exercise without mistakes.

C ! Anwendung von *present perfect progressive*

Längere Handlungen, die	
in der Vergangenheit begannen und „hier und jetzt“ noch immer andauern.	in der Vergangenheit begannen und erst vor kurzem zu Ende gingen.
„schon seit“ (mit Gegenwart)	**„die ganze Zeit“** (mit Vergangenheit)
I've been looking for Joe for days. *I have no idea where he could be.*	***I've been looking for you all day.*** *Here you are at last!*
Ich suche ihn schon seit Tagen (und habe ihn noch immer nicht gefunden).	Ich habe dich den ganzen Tag gesucht (aber da bist du ja endlich).

D ! „schon seit“ mit *since* und *for*

Present perfect progressive sagt oft, **seit wann oder wie lange schon** eine Handlung andauert.

seit	
seit einer bestimmten Zeit bis „hier und jetzt“ → **Zeitpunkt**	eine bestimmte Zeit lang bis „hier und jetzt“ → **Zeitspanne**
since	***for***
since midnight	*for five seconds*
since 10 a.m.	*for ten hours*
since yesterday	*for a week*
since 2010	*for some months*
since my birthday	*for a long time*
since the Roman Age	*for ever*

E !! Unterschiede zwischen *present perfect simple* und *progressive*

simple	*progressive*
Zustände	**Handlungen**
We've been here for a week now.	*We've been staying here since Friday.*
I've known Julia since kindergarden.	*I've been writing to Julia for years.*
Handlungen, die schon sehr lange andauern	**Handlungen, die noch nicht so lange andauern**
My family has lived here for ever.	*Betty has been living here since 2012.*
I think we have waited long enough!	*I've been waiting for you for an hour.*
Auswirkung, Folge, Ergebnis	
This is an excellent film. I've seen it three times already.	
Have you seen Gloria lately? – Yes, she looks horrible with her pink hair.	

127 Fill in present perfect progressive.

EXAMPLE Jimmy, *I have been waiting* (*wait*) for you for ages!

1. Sue's really tired because she .... (*jog*) for almost an hour.
2. How long .... (*you/work*) on this homework?
3. Paul .... (*sleep*) for nearly 18 hours. That's not normal!
4. This terrible noise .... (*go*) on all night.
5. The boys .... (*play*) soccer for two hours.
6. .... (*study*) English all day long, Eve?
7. At the moment there is an interesting football match on TV: Austria versus Sweden. Timmy .... (*watch*) since the beginning.

128 Fill in *for* or *since*.

EXAMPLE I'm very proud because I haven't eaten any sweets *for* a week.

1. Have you ever managed not to check your Facebook account .... more than two days? I think that's impossible!
2. Gerti has had her Facebook account .... the beginning of May.
3. .... when have you known the truth, Howard?
4. Kate and Peter have been a couple .... Christmas last year.
5. I have loved doing sports .... almost all my life.
6. Nora hasn't received any messages .... yesterday afternoon.
7. I have had the same VW Golf .... ten years now.
8. Rick hasn't eaten mashed potatoes .... his childhood.
9. .... how long have you been working on your diploma?
10. .... when have you not been in touch with Roberta?
11. Charlotte has had her iPhone .... her last birthday.
12. Mum, I have been trying to call you .... a quarter of an hour!
13. Jessica hasn't been to school .... her cold started last Tuesday.
14. Gilbert has been trying to fall asleep .... hours, but he can't.

129 ! Present perfect simple or progressive?

Lewis: *Have you already seen* *(you/already/see)* Maisie today? She looks cool because she ______ *(be)* to the hairdresser, and the new haircut suits her very well.

Greg: No, but that reminds me of the fact that I ______ *(not/see)* my hairdresser for ages. I'd better make an appointment soon.

Lewis: Yes, you'd better, because I ______ *(not/be)* able to see your face for quite a while with all that hair.

Greg: You're right. That's because I ______ *(try)* to grow my hair for almost a year. I thought it would look cool but …

Lewis: … but somehow it doesn't, sorry. ______ *(you/ever/think)* about shaving your hair off completely?

Greg: Hell no!! Why should I? I ______ *(never/like)* bald people! They look as if they were ill.

Lewis: You think so? I think they look smashing! Besides, many famous people ______ *(shave)* off their hair, and now they are even more popular.

Greg: Really? I ______ *(never/hear)* of a star who's shaved off his hair and become famous. Anyway, I feel like we ______ *(talk)* about this weird topic way too long! So let's move on to something more interesting. What about the FIFA game you ordered last week? ______ *(it/already/arrive)* or are you still waiting?

Lewis: No, it ______ *(not/arrive)* yet, though I ______ *(wait)* for it for days! But I desperately hope to get it before the weekend!

Greg: Well, I ______ *(never/order)* anything online, but call me when it arrives so we can play together!

F !! Unterschied zwischen *past simple* und *present perfect simple*

Für Deutsch Sprechende ist dieser Unterschied nicht immer leicht verständlich. Es gibt im Deutschen keine großen Unterschiede zwischen:

„Ich **verlor** meinen Schülerausweis."
Oder „Ich **habe** meinen Schülerausweis **verloren**."

Im Englischen ist das anders. Es ist nicht egal, ob man sagt:

*I **lost** my student card.*	*I **have lost** my student card.*
past simple	***present perfect simple***
Der Satz in ***past simple*** bedeutet einfach, dass ich **irgendwann einmal** den Ausweis verlor – vielleicht gestern, vielleicht voriges Jahr, vielleicht vor zehn Jahren. Er sagt nichts darüber aus, ob ich ihn je wieder fand oder nicht. Wir erfahren etwas über das **„Damals"** und nicht über das „Hier und Jetzt".	Der Satz in ***present perfect simple*** besagt, dass ich „hier und jetzt" keinen Ausweis mehr habe, weil ich ihn verloren habe. Dabei ist es ganz **egal, wann** das passierte; von Interesse ist nur, **dass** es passiert ist. Wir erfahren etwas über das **„Hier und Jetzt"** – nämlich, dass mein Ausweis weg ist!
damals	**seit damals – hier und jetzt**
*Agatha Christie **wrote** 66 detective stories.* (Sie starb 1976. Sie kann daher keine Kriminalromane mehr schreiben.)	*Wolf **Haas has written** seven detective stories.* (Bis jetzt! Kann ja sein, dass er noch weitere Kriminalromane schreiben wird.)
*In 1605, the first European settlers **arrived** in America.*	*Since then, millions of people from all over the world **have followed** them.*
*I **lost** my student card last week, …* *Dad **came** home an hour ago, …*	*… and I **haven't found** it yet.* *… but he **hasn't had** dinner yet.*

ACHTUNG – Nur *present perfect simple* bei …

- **negativen Aussagen** → *I **haven't seen** you in a very long time.*
  *My grandma **has never been** to England.*
- **bestimmten Verben** → *I'**ve wanted** to see this film for ages.*
  *We'**ve known** the Jacksons since we moved to this neighbourhood.*
  *My parents **have** always **believed** in me.*
  *No more Coke, thanks! I'**ve had** enough!*
  *This land **has belonged** to us for ever.*

believe	*have*	*love*	*realise*	*see*
belong	*hear*	*mean*	*recognise*	*seem*
forget	*know*	*need*	*remember*	*want*
hate	*like*	*prefer*	*understand*	*wish*

130 ! Past tense or present perfect tense – complete!

Roger: Hi, James, nice to see you! Is this your new car?

James: Hi Roger! Yes, it is. It looks fantastic, doesn't it?

Roger: Yes, it does! How long **have you had** (*you/have*) it?

James: I .... (*get*) it last Thursday.

Roger: Wow, so it's REALLY brand new! Why .... (*you/decide*) to get a BMW?

James: You see, I .... (*always/want*) to have a BMW and then I .... (*have*) the chance to get one. My brother-in-law .... (*sell*) it to me at a good price.

Roger: Sounds great! Why .... (*he/sell*) it?

James: He .... (*not/use*) it much any more. You see some time ago he .... (*realise*) that going to work by train is easier and more relaxing.

Roger: That's true. He seems to be a really clever person!

James: Yes, he absolutely is, and he .... (*always/be*) like that. Tell me, Roger, ... (*you/ever/think*) of selling your car and taking the train to work, too?

Roger: Honestly, no. I love driving and I .... (*never/feel*) the desire to go by train. Last month I .... (*have*) to take my car to the garage so I .... (*must*) take the train and it .... (*be*) horrible.

James: I know what you mean. I .... (*really/be*) very happy since I .... (*buy*) the car.

Roger: Well, if you're so happy I'm sure it .... (*be*) a good decision! I hope you'll never have an accident with it! Bye, James, and have a nice day!

131 !! Past tense or present perfect tense – translate!

EXAMPLE Hast du dir schon den neuen *Daft Punk*-Song heruntergeladen?
Have you already downloaded the new Daft Punk song?

1. Ja, das habe ich letzte Woche gemacht.

2. Sharon hat seit über einer Woche das Internet nicht benützt.

3. Caroline hat noch nie einen süßeren Burschen kennengelernt.

4. Bist du letzten Samstag in den *Hollister*-Shop gegangen?

5. Hast du *Hangover 3* letztes Wochenende gesehen?

6. Ich war seit über einem Monat nicht mehr im Kino.

7. Hat Moni schon für die Latein-Schularbeit gelernt?

132 ! Past or present perfect – find the correct questions.

EXAMPLE *How long have you been waiting for Ben's email?*
I have been waiting for Ben's email for half an hour.

1. ?

She bought her MacBook two years ago.

2. ?

No, sorry, Mum, I haven't done my homework yet.

3. ?

Unfortunately, I have not. But I would like to go to Canada this year.

4. ?

No, I haven't answered Mike's message because I don't know what to tell him.

TENSES: *PAST PERFECT TENSE* – VORVERGANGENHEIT, PLUSQUAMPERFEKT

A Formen von *past perfect tense*

past perfect simple	*past perfect progressive*
active	
had asked alle Personen → ***had + 3rd form***	***had been asking*** alle Personen → ***had been + ing-form***
passive	
had been asked	–

B ! Anwendung von *past perfect*

- *Past perfect* ist die Vergangenheit von *past* und *present perfect*. Dies zeigt sich in der indirekten Rede (*reported speech*, ab Seite 116).

  *Joe said, "It **was raining** when I **left** the house this morning."*
  *Joe said it **had been raining** when **he had left** the house that morning.*
  *Tina said, "We **haven't seen** Max in a long time."*
  *Tina said they **hadn't seen** Max in a long time.*

- *Past perfect* zeigt, welche Handlung (von zwei oder mehreren) vor der (oder den) anderen geschehen ist. Diese frühere Handlung war schon beendet, als die spätere begann. Die Reihenfolge im Satz – früher/später oder später/früher – ist dabei egal.

  I had shut the curtains and (had) locked the door before I went to bed.

frühere Handlungen	spätere Handlung
↓	↓
past perfect	*past*

  When Joe called last night, we had already left the house and gone to town.

spätere Handlung	frühere Handlungen
↓	↓
past	*past perfect*

- ***Past perfect progressive*** verwendet man, um zu zeigen, wie lange eine Handlung schon andauerte, bevor eine zweite geschah.

  The men had been shouting for help all night before someone heard them.
  The war had been going on for years when peace finally came.
  After Scott had been struggling with difficulties all the way, he reached the South Pole a month after Amundsen.

↓	↓	↓
länger andauernde, „ältere" Handlung (*past perfect*)	Zeitdauer	später dazukommende Handlung (*past*)

- ***Past perfect*** kommt im ***third conditional*** – dem Fall der Unmöglichkeit – in den Bedingungen vor. Siehe dazu auch Seite 32.

*If the weather **had been** better, we **would have gone** to the mountains.*
*The Pilgrims **would have starved** if the natives **had not helped** them to survive.*
*How **would** you **have reacted** if you **had known** the truth from the start?*

133 Fill in past perfect tense.

EXAMPLE When I came home I found out that I **had left** (*vergessen*) my English books at school. So I couldn't do the homework.

1. After Shannon ______________ (*anrufen*) Max, she still had to wait for almost half an hour until he arrived.
2. Eve wanted to unlock her car when she realised that she ______________ (*verlieren*) her key. What bad luck!
3. Before I wrote my English essay I ______________ (*lesen*) an article on *Wikipedia* to inform myself, which was quite interesting.
4. After Maurice ______________ (*kaufen*) the tickets for the *Urban Art Forms* festival in Styria, he was very happy and excited.
5. If I ______________ (*wissen/kennen*) the truth, I really would not have helped you, Joseph!
6. Carl is such an unreliable person, because after I ______________ (*borgen*) him some money, I never got it back! That's really unfair!
7. After DJ Antoine ______________ (*herausbringen/veröffentlichen*) his dance hit *Ma Cherie*, he became an internationally recognised star.
8. Tina unpacked all her things after she ______________ (*move*) into her new apartment. That was quite a lot of work!
9. Victor and his friends were rather disappointed after they ______________ (*anschauen*) the new Bond movie *Skyfall*. If they ______________ (*wissen*) it was going to be so awful, they would have gone to Selina's party instead!
10. After I ______________ (*machen*) all the exercises, I understood the correct use of the English tenses.

134 ! Past or past perfect – circle the correct option!

EXAMPLE I *worked* / *had worked* hard, that's why I *got* / *had got* good grades.

1. Yesterday Chris *met* / *had met* a girl that he *never saw* / *had never seen* before.
2. *Did you go* / *Had you gone* home after you *left* / *had left* the party?
3. It *was* / *had been* Peter's birthday last weekend, so Belinda *baked* / *had baked* a tasty chocolate cake the day before.
4. After Tim *installed* / *had installed* the anti-virus programme, the computer *broke* / *had broken* down.
5. What *did you do* / *had you done* after Nora *split up* / *had split up* with you?
6. The dog *smelled* / *had smelled* better after it *was* / *had been* thoroughly cleaned.
7. After Sonja *reached* / *had reached* the peak of the mountain, she *felt* / *had felt* extremely happy and proud of herself because she *never climbed* / *had never climbed* a more difficult mountain before.
8. Silly Melanie! She *ate up* / *had eaten up* all the creamy doughnuts and then she *felt* / *had felt* sick.
9. What bad luck! When James *arrived* / *had arrived* at the airport he *realised* / *had realised* that he *forgot* / *had forgotten* his passport at home.
10. After I *watched* / *had watched* the film, I *was* / *had been* tired and sleepy.
11. After Claire *bought* / *had bought* her first car, she *didn't have* / *hadn't had* any money left. So she *started* / *had started* looking for a job.
12. What *did you do* / *had you done* after you *finished* / *had finished* school?
13. Clarissa *was* / *had been* a nurse before she *realised* / *had realised* that she *didn't want* / *hadn't wanted* to do this job any longer.
14. I *studied* / *had studied* the past perfect thoroughly before I *did* / *had done* this task.
15. Before dad's car *was taken* / *had been taken* to the garage, he *washed* / *had washed* it.
16. After he *kissed* / *had kissed* her, he *went* / *had gone* home happily.
17. The new dresses *were washed* / *had been washed* before they *were put away* / *had been put* away.

TENSES: FUTURE TENSE – ZUKUNFT

A *future with "will"* – Die Zukunft mit *will*

- Wird i**n allen Personen** der Ein- und Mehrzahl auf die gleiche Weise gebildet:

  will (not)* + *infinitive *(base form)*
  *I **will** always **remember** you. – George **will be** famous one day.*
  *We **won't be** here next week. – **Will** they **come** again?*

- Wird verwendet **für Ereignisse, über die man keine wirkliche Kontrolle hat**: Annahmen, Erwartungen, Hoffnung, Versprechen, Vorhersagen; oft erkennbar an Wörtern wie ***think, hope, expect, suppose*** oder ***maybe, perhaps, probably***.

  *Our coach **thinks** we'**ll win** the championship this year.*
  *I **hope** I **won't disappoint** you!*
  *They **will probably ask** for our ID cards at the door.*

- Wird auch verwendet bei **plötzlichen Entscheidungen** („ohne viel nachzudenken"):

  *Today is Laura's birthday. – What? I almost forgot. I'**ll get** her a present at once.*
  *I can't open this bottle! – Give it to me. I'**ll show** you!*

B *future with "going to"* – Die Zukunft mit *going to*

- Wird mit ***am/is/are* + *going to* + *infinitive*** gebildet:

  *I'**m going to tell** you a strange story.*
  *Sue **is going to get** married! She's just told me so.*
  *They **are** finally **going to repair** the bridge!*

- Wird verwendet **bei festen Absichten** und **Vorhaben**:

  *We'**re not going to disappoint** you!*
  ***Are** you **going to come** to my party, Harry?*
  *Max and I **are going to start** a punk band.*

- Wird verwendet **für Ereignisse, die unmittelbar bevorstehen** (egal ob geplant oder unbeabsichtigt) → **nahe Zukunft** / *near future*:

  *You'**re going to see** something unbelieveable now.*
  *Look at this man! He'**s going to jump** from the bridge!*
  *Put on a warm coat; it'**s going to get** very cold.*

- Mit ***was/were going to*** … **für Handlungen**, die geplant waren, aber **nicht durchgeführt** wurden:

  *I **was going to call** you, but then I forgot. I'm sorry!*
  *Betty and Steve **were going to come** tonight, but Betty got sick.*
  *We **weren't going to stay**, but they insisted, and so we did.*

C *present progressive* mit zukünftiger Bedeutung

- Für fest geplante (zukünftige) Ereignisse, für die schon ein Zeitpunkt feststeht:

*When **are** you **leaving** for Canada? – Next Tuesday.*
*Tina **is having** a party on Saturday. Are you going?*
*I'**m meeting** Brian and Judy after school. Do you want to come?*

D *present simple* mit zukünftiger Bedeutung

- Vorwiegend für Angaben im Zusammenhang mit Zeitplänen, Fahrplänen, Stundenplänen, Öffnungszeiten usw.

*Brian's bus **leaves** in half an hour.*
*The next lecture **begins** at two o'clock.*
*Our first lesson tomorrow **is** French.*
*Dad's plane **arrives** tonight.*

E ! *future progressive*

- In allen Personen der Ein- und Mehrzahl: ***will be + ing-form***
- Wird für Handlungen verwendet, die zu einem zukünftigen Zeitpunkt gerade im Gang sein werden:

***At this time of day tomorrow**, Joe **will be taking** a nap, I **will be watching** TV, and the children **will be playing** outside.*

F Für *future passive* siehe Seite 88.

ACHTUNG!

Welche Form der Zukunft man verwendet, hängt davon ab, was man zum Ausdruck bringen will – eine Erwartung etwa oder eine feste Absicht oder eine Vorhersage; oder man will auf ein knapp bevorstehendes Ereignis hinweisen.
Es kann daher – je nach dem Sinn der Aussage – mehr als eine „richtige" Lösung geben!

135 ! **Read the dialogue and fill in the correct future tenses.**

Lisa: Hey Jenny, summer holidays **are coming** *(come)* up soon. Have you got any plans already?

Jenny: Well, I'm not absolutely sure what I ______________ *(do)*. I ______________ *(definitely/stay)* at home in the first week because I need to relax for a while.

Lisa: Yes, I know what you mean! I'm quite exhausted as well from all the stress we had at school during the last few weeks.

Jenny: That's true. In the last two weeks I kept telling myself, "Keep going, Jenny! You ______________ *(manage)* all this."

Lisa: And did it help?

Jenny: Well … sometimes it did, and sometimes it doesn't. What about your summer holidays, by the way?

Lisa: I ______________ *(go)* to Mexico in July.

Jenny: Wow, that sounds fantastic! Tell me more about it!

Lisa: We ______________ *(leave)* on the 14th of July and we ______________ *(return)* at the beginning of August. We ______________ *(visit)* Mexico City, Merida and Cancún. I hope it ______________ *(be)* exciting and fun.

Jenny: I'm sure it ______________ *(be)*! I wish I could go with you!

Lisa: Unfortunately our plane ______________ *(take off)* at 3:00 in the morning so we ______________ *(must)* get up very early. But I'd say it is worth it!

Jenny: I really envy you, Lisa. ______________ *(you/send)* me a postcard from your trip?

Lisa: Of course! … I hope I ______________ *(not forget)* it. Enjoy your summer, Jenny! See you in September!

136 ! Fill in the correct future tenses.

EXAMPLE Today temperatures should rise up to 37 degrees so I am sure that I'***m going to eat*** *(essen)* an ice cream in the afternoon.

1. The train .... *(abfahren/wegfahren)* at a quarter past six, doesn't it?
2. I .... *(senden/schicken)* you an email but then my mobile rang and I somehow forgot to do it.
3. Christine, you really need a trendier haircut! I .... *(machen)* an appointment for you right now!
4. Mum, I think I .... *(haben/nehmen)* the cheeseburger and some fries, please.
5. Next Saturday .... *(sein)* Tom's birthday. He .... *(haben)* a big party – he has already invited all his close friends, but he hasn't done the shopping yet. Perhaps he .... *(machen)* it today. I'm sure the party .... *(sein)* great fun!
6. I hope I .... *(schaffen/durchkommen)* the English test because if not, I .... *(probably/müssen)* repeat the 6th form.
7. The English lesson .... *(enden)* at ten past ten and the history lesson .... *(beginnen)* five minutes later.
8. Eve and John .... *(heiraten)* next month – on the 21st of March. They .... *(feiern)* a big party with their families and all their close friends.
9. Oh no, look at that!! My laptop has finally stopped working! I .... *(müssen/kaufen)* a new one as soon as possible or else I .... *(nicht können/arbeiten)* for school.
10. I hope I .... *(niemals/erleben)* something like this again!

MIXED TENSES

137 ! Mixed tenses: Which tenses do these signal words usually indicate?

EXAMPLE yesterday *past simple tense*

1. recently ....
2. two days ago ....
3. after ....
4. now ....
5. for ....
6. all my life ....
7. before ....
8. next Monday ....
9. just ....
10. at this moment ....
11. upcoming holidays ....
12. lately ....
13. last month ....
14. always ....
15. already ....

138 ! Put the following verbs into the given tense.

EXAMPLE wir zahlen *(past simple)* *we paid*

1. sie fängt *(present perfect simple)* ....
2. ich falle *(will-future)* ....
3. er verkauft *(present simple)* ....
4. du siehst *(past perfect simple)* ....
5. ihr wartet *(present perfect progressive)* ....
6. es wird *(present progressive)* ....
7. sie leben *(past perfect progressive)* ....

139 ! Which tense is it? Write down the names of the tenses.

EXAMPLE they had been dancing *past perfect progressive*

1. I was reading ....
2. we have been studying ....
3. he is reading ....
4. you did ....
5. she is going to dance ....
6. it had rained ....
7. she sleeps ....

140 ! Mixed tenses: Find the correct questions – mind the tenses.

EXAMPLE *How long have you been studying for the final exam?*
I have been studying for the final exam for almost six weeks.

1. ....?
   She bought the car from a friend of her brother's.
2. ....?
   Oh yes, she is growing tomatoes and cucumbers this year.
3. ....?
   He eats at McDonald's once or twice a week, that's quite a lot I'd say.
4. ....?
   They were waiting for their teacher for fifteen minutes.

141 !! Translate the sentences. Mind the correct tense.

EXAMPLE Bitte störe mich nicht, denn ich mache gerade meine Hausübung.
Please don't disturb me because I am doing my homework (at the moment).

1. Bist du schon jemals in Irland gewesen?
   ....
2. Du musst mir glauben, dass ich Irina nicht angerufen habe!
   ....
3. Leider versteht sie nicht Französisch.
   ....
4. Charles, was hast du gestern um viertel neun am Abend gemacht?
   ....
5. Ich fürchte mich vor Hunden, seitdem mich einer gebissen hat.
   ....
6. Newman hat noch nicht das Abendessen gekocht.
   ....
7. Gestern musste ich nicht so früh ins Bett gehen.
   ....

142 ! **Banked gap fill: Read through the email and decide which verbs you need. Write your answers in the space provided. There are two extra verbs which you don't need. The first one (0) has been done for you.**

To: tobi.maquire@yahoo.uk
From: jeremy2010@hotmail.com
Subject: Greetings from Carinthia

Hi Tobi,

How are you? I **(0)** ______ you are as well as I am at the moment but somehow I doubt it! I **(1)** ______ here in Carinthia, Austria, with my class for about six days and it's simply amazing. We **(2)** ______ a sports week, which means that we exercise every day and have a lot of fun!

We **(3)** ______ last Monday. The bus ride, which took almost fifteen hours, was rather boring, but when we saw our apartments, the strenuous journey **(4)** ______. I share a room with my best friends, Jason and Carl, and we even have a balcony overlooking Maltschacher Lake. That's a very small lake close to Klagenfurt but it's really nice here. The girls from our class stay in the neighbouring house, so they aren't far away if you know what I mean... ;-)

As I have already mentioned, we exercise every day. Back at home we **(5)** ______ from a range of sports (like tennis, beach volleyball, sailing, surfing, biking, and many more), and we have one sports session in the morning and one in the afternoon. I **(6)** ______ mountainbiking and I play tennis, as I have never done so before. The tennis instructor is very good and he **(7)** ______ things very well. The biking guide is not that good, he sometimes appears a bit lazy.

Anyway, the food is awesome and very tasty, especially lunch and dinner. In the afternoon there is usually a snack with some fruit and cake, and we can also get something to drink any time we want to. Fortunately the teachers **(8)** ______ very relaxed. Sometimes they join in our sports activities, but often they do other sports like jogging or they simply sit by the lake and read.

We **(9)** ______ here for another three days and then we'll go back home. I hope things are alright with you and that you have passed the biology test you were so worried about. See you soon, mate, and all the best!

Jeremy

A	are	**B**	are having	**C**	are staying
D	arrived	**E**	chose	**F**	could choose
G	explains	**H**	had arrived	**I**	have been
J	*hope*	**K**	is explaining	**L**	was forgotten

0	1	2	3	4	5	6	7	8	9
J									

143 ! **Banked gap fill: Read this weblog about agility and put the verbs into the correct tenses. Also, fill in the adjectives/adverbs from the list below. Write the letters (A–L) in the space provided. There is one extra word which you do not need. The first one (0) has been done for you.**

Hi, my name is Amy. I **started** *(starten/anfangen)* this weblog in order to inform you about the progress I .... *(schon/machen)* and .... *(hoffentlich/machen)* in the future with my dog Justin concerning our agility training. I .... *(bekommen)* Justin as a nine-week-old pup. He is an Australian Shepherd, and I have to say that he is a real beauty. His fur is white, grey and brown, and he .... *(haben)* one blue eye and one brown eye. That makes him look very **(0)** ...... and interesting.

*

The first weeks with Justin were quite exhausting and **(1)** ...... because he followed me everywhere I .... *(gehen)*. Just imagine – I .... *(nichteinmal/können)* to the loo without him running after me. Luckily this .... *(sich bessern)* a lot by now and we .... *(nicht/haben)* any **(2)** ...... problems in this respect. We go for walks every day, and each of them .... *(andauern)* for at least three quarters of an hour. Justin .... *(lieben)* running around in the woods, and he always .... *(wollen)* me to throw sticks for him to .... *(fangen)* and bring back. I think I could do that **(3)** ....

*

Now Justin is already 18 weeks old and he .... *(wachsen)* **(4)** .... I .... *(lehren/beibringen)* him some simple tricks which he is able to .... *(ausführen)* **(5)** .... A few days ago, however, one of my friends asked me why I .... *(nicht/machen)* agility with Justin. I .... *(niemals/hören)* about that before so my friend explained it to me. He told me that it .... *(sein)* a sports programme for dogs that combines balance, coordination, speed, strength and endurance. He also said that Australian Shepherds (or Aussies, as they are often called) .... *(sein)* particularly talented for that kind of training as they are a **(6)** ...... clever breed. I said that I would think about it, and on the same day I .... *(konsultieren)* the Internet for some more information.

Yesterday Justin and I ______________ *(haben)* our first agility training and I must say that (at least for me) it was a bit confusing, but also fun. It's a simple training course that we ______________ *(tun/machen)* at the moment because Justin is still very young, but I really had the impression that he ______________ *(genießen)* the obstacle course. I had to shout instructions and commands at him and he had to jump over various obstacles, balance on some sort of ladder and crawl through **(7)** ______ tunnels. The training lasted an hour, and in the end both of us were **(8)** ______ . After I ______________ *(fangen)* my breath again, the agility instructor came over to me and ______________ *(sagen)* that we ______________ *(tun/machen)* a great job. Of course I was very proud of Justin, so I ______________ *(beschließen)* to continue with the training.

*

Wow, time ______________ *(vergehen/gehen)* by so quickly! Now Justin ______________ *(fast/erreichen)* his full adult size. His fur is very thick and **(9)** ______ and he is in really good shape. I love him very much and he his definitely the best that ______________ *(jemals/passieren, geschehen)* in my life!!! We still do agility **(10)** ______, usually twice a week, and I have to say it's really cool. The tasks Justin has to do ______________ *(werden)* more difficult recently but he still manages them without any problems. Unfortunately the training ______________ *(in Anspruch nehmen)* quite a lot of my time, that's why I ______________ *(beschließen)* to stop writing this weblog. Justin and I are ______________ *(sicherlich/fortsetzen)* our agility training because during the last few months it ______________ *(werden)* an integral part of both our lives!!

So long and all the best, Amy & Justin :-)

A	endlessly	**B**	exhausted	**C**	narrow
D	particularly	**E**	perfectly	**F**	proudly
G	regularly	**H**	serious	**I**	shiny
J	significantly	**K**	**special**	**L**	tiring

0	1	2	3	4	5	6	7	8	9	10
K										

144 ! Editing: Rihanna – Drunk in Bar

You are going to read a text about Rihanna. In some of the lines there is a tense mistake. Find it and write down the correct version in the space provided. Some lines are okay. Indicate these with ✔ a. The first ones (00), (0) have been done for you.

Rihanna – Drunk in Bar

She **is** obviously one of the most successful female pop and	(00)	✔
RnB singers of recent times. So far she **had sold** 37 million	(0)	has sold
albums and her songs have downloaded online about 146	(1)	
million times. Besides, she had been awarded seven Grammy	(2)	
Awards. Rihanna has always been being a very hard working	(3)	
singer who concentrates and focuses on her career, her	(4)	
success and her image. But this obviously has changed	(5)	
at the beginning of summer 2013.	(6)	
On March 18th, 2013, the singer is starting her new *Diamonds*	(7)	
World Tour featuring the album *Unapologetic*. The tour lasted	(8)	
until November 2013 and saw the singer perform on five	(9)	
continents all over the world. All in all she gives 94 concerts.	(10)	
In July 2013, in times when she should have focus on her	(11)	
work most, however, she suddenly begins to appear in	(12)	
newspapers headlines with shocking and negative news like	(13)	
"Rihanna Drunk in Bar". As a consequence, a lot of negative	(14)	
publicity had been created. But that was not the worst.	(15)	
In addition, the queen of modern pop was staying out all night	(16)	
long, forgot the lyrics of her own songs when she was on	(17)	
stage, hitted a fanatic fan with a microphone and even had to	(18)	
postpone the beginning of her concerts as she was not sober	(19)	
enough for a live performance. Most of her fans at the	(20)	
concerts were extremely angry and disappointed after	(21)	
Rihanna made them wait for almost an eternity. "I would say	(22)	
this was definitely and irrevocably the last Rihanna concert I	(23)	
went to", said Roger Bertrand angrily after the beginning of a	(24)	
concert had postponed again and again.	(25)	
No doubt, Rihanna's behaviour had become unacceptable.	(26)	
That's also what her manager was thinking and therefore he	(27)	
sent her an e-mail, urgently asking her to check her manners	(28)	
and changing her behaviour.	(29)	
Let's just hope that in future Rihanna would not go on ruining	(30)	
her career and living her life according to the title of her own	(31)	
song, *Good Girl Gone Bad*.	(32)	

145 ! **Read through the dialogue and complete it with the verbs in the correct tense.**

Jasmin: Hey, Lola! Now that some weeks of our summer holidays ***have already passed*** *(already/pass)*, tell me what ______ *(you/do)* so far? I'm very curious!

Lola: Well, I ______ *(have)* a really great time so far. You see, at the beginning of the holidays I ______ *(go)* to some festivals in Austria with some friends.

Jasmin: Really? Which festivals ______ *(you/go)* to?

Lola: The first one ______ *(be)* *Nova Rock* in Burgenland. As I ______ *(never/be)* to an event like that, I had my doubts at first. But after my friends ______ *(convince)* me to come along, I was really happy and I ______ *(be)* terribly sad if I had missed this awesome event. My favourite band, *Thirty Seconds to Mars*, performed on the Friday, and they were terrific!

Jasmin: This really ______ *(sound)* great. I wish I ______ *(be)* there, too! And the other events?

Lola: Just one – the *Urban Art Festival* in Graz. It ______ *(take)* place in July also, and it ______ *(last)* from Friday to Sunday as well. A friend of mine ______ *(rent)* a caravan for the weekend, so we ______ *(can/all/sleep)* in it and it was really fun, I can tell you! And honestly, if anybody ______ *(tell)* me that you can sleep so soundly in a thing like that, I wouldn't ______ *(believe)* it!

Jasmin: What a pity I wasn't with you! But maybe I ______ *(join)* you next year if you go there again!

Lola: You do that, Jasmin! It ______ *(be)* great if you could come with us!

146 !! **Banked gap fill: Read this interview with Mrs Joan Bead, an expert on contemporary literature. Complete the text with the verbs in the correct tense and form – you find the infinitives in the box at the end. Remember – there is one verb you should not use!**

Interviewer: Mrs Bead, you ***have been studying*** the phenomenon of "Harry Potter" for a long time. Would you be so kind as to ______________ some questions related to the topic?

Mrs Bead: Yes, of course. It would be a pleasure!

Interviewer: What can you tell us about the Harry Potter books?

Mrs Bead: Well, the first novel of the series was *Harry Potter and the Philosopher's Stone*. It ______________ in 1997, by Bloomsbury Publishing in London, England. The complete series ______________ seven novels, which all deal with the adventures of Harry Potter and his friends, Ronald Weasley and Hermione Granger.

Interviewer: How successful is the Harry Potter series?

Mrs Bead: It's been an unbelievable commercial success worldwide, and the books ______________ into 67 languages. I ______________ the series has even set a record as the fastest-selling books in history, but I'm not sure about that.

Interviewer: What is the storyline, actually?

Mrs Bead: As I ______________ before, it's about the adventures of Harry Potter and his friends. Harry is an orphan, whose parents ______________ in a car accident. He ______________ that he is a wizard and ______________ magical powers. Each of the novels ______________ one year in Harry's life, and their set-up is usually similar: Harry and his friends have to face dangerous situations while fighting evil. In doing so, they often end up breaking school rules, but learn moral lessons. The stories ______________ from a third person point of view.

Interviewer: Which genre do the novels belong to?

Mrs Bead: That's an interesting question. Strictly speaking, they belong to the category of fantasy, but they also ……………………………… elements of mystery, thriller and romance.

Interviewer: What about the series' main themes?

Mrs Bead: Well, the focus ……………………………… clearly on the topic of death. But apart from that, the novels also deal with ordinary teenage challenges such as friendship, peer-pressure and school life. They are definitely about growing up and developing one's individual personality. That's why they are suitable both for kids and teens. But not exclusively, of course.

Interviewer: What about the Harry Potter film versions?

Mrs Bead: I ……………………………… any of them yet, but they ……………………………… to be exciting and very well made.

Interviewer: Mrs Bead, what would you do if you ……………………………… Harry Potter face to face?

Mrs Bead: Well, let me ……………………………… ! If I really had the chance, I ……………………………… him to perform a trick with his magic wand!

Interviewer: Fantastic. Thanks a lot for answering all my questions, Mrs Bead! It ……………………… most interesting and instructive to talk to you!

☐	to answer	☐	to find out	☐	to say
☐	to ask	☐	to forget	☐	to see
☐	to be	☐	to have	✔	to study
☐	to be	☐	to include	☐	to tell
☐	to comprise	☐	to meet	☐	to think
☐	to cover	☐	to mention	☐	to think
☐	to die	☐	to publish	☐	to translate

147 !! Editing: How to Deal with Breakups

You are going to read a text about breakups and how to handle them. In some of the lines there is a word that should not be there. Find it and write it down in the spaces provided. Some lines are okay. Indicate these with a ✔. The first ones (00, 0) have been done for you.

How to Deal with Breakups

It's a process I'm sure everyone has already gone through, some	(00)	✔
just once, **the** others more often: falling in love. It's probably the	(0)	the
most amazing and wonderful feeling in the world and one that	(1)	
should – if we were to be choose – never stop. You feel like flying	(2)	
all over the time, you seem to be in a good mood non-stop and you	(3)	
could not embrace the whole world. It's simply indescribable!	(4)	
Unfortunately, this feeling does not last for ever and after such an	(5)	
emotional high, you often crash-land on the hard ground of all	(6)	
reality: the breakup.	(7)	
Splitting up with your partner is never an as easy thing to do, no	(8)	
matter how long the relationship has lasted. There is also no	(9)	
scientific evidence whether men or women suffer from more when	(10)	
it comes to the breaking up. What is clear, though, is that women	(11)	
suffer differently and are more likely to communicate their loss and	(12)	
loneliness, while few men keep their feelings and disappointment	(13)	
to themselves.	(14)	
Anyway, what most people who concerned would need in a	(15)	
situation like this is a recipe of how to handle with the breakup and	(16)	
the their related consequences. But it goes without saying that	(17)	
such a general recipe doesn't exist yet and in a fact everybody has	(18)	
to find out for themselves which actions help and which increase	(19)	
and intensify your suffering instead.	(20)	
As a rule, it's always of a good idea to remove photos showing you	(21)	
and your partner together as they would however only remind you	(22)	
constantly of what you don't have got any longer: a happy and loving	(23)	
relationship. At next, put away your partner's belongings and try	(24)	
to accept that – in a way – a new life lies ahead of you. Always	(25)	
think positively and don't just stay at his home hoping your	(26)	
partner might do return to you, telling you that he or she can't live	(27)	
without you. This scenario is more than unlikely to have happen.	(28)	
Finally, accept the new situation and don't only think about the	(29)	
"good old days". Don't compare between your former partner with	(30)	
people you will meet in the future. There was a reason why you	(31)	
and your partner split up with, so don't seek your ex-partner's	(32)	
characteristics in the next new people you will meet!	(33)	

148 !! Open gap fill: Horrible Birthday Party

Read the following report about a birthday party that went completely out of control. In some sentences the verb is missing. Fill it in at the bottom but take care to use a meaningful verb in the correct tense! The first one (0) has been done for you.

Horrible Birthday Party

Last Saturday night Jason N. (18) and his girlfriend Samona B. (16) **(0)** ______ their birthdays at the well-known *Estate Club* in Warwick. Long before that, they had prepared invitation cards and distributed them among their friends. All in all, they **(1)** ______ about 25 people and everybody **(2)** ______ forward to an amusing and entertaining evening full of laughter and fun.

Jason and Samona arrived at the club at about 9 p.m. and soon their friends showed up as well, one after the other. They all hugged, expressing birthday wishes and exchanging gifts. The mood **(3)** ______ jolly and good. But suddenly one of Jason's friends came with the news that there **(4)** ______ about 65 people outside the club, waiting to get in and join the party.

It **(5)** ______ long for the crowd of young people to enter the club and crash the party. None of them **(6)** ______ and none of them was a friend of any of the guests. In fact, nobody knew them at all, but obviously they were a bunch of wild and most probably drunk youths looking for trouble – which they soon found.

One of the drunk teens threatened Jason with a knife, and when Samona **(7)** ______ that, she wanted to intervene. Then things **(8)** ______ out of hand very quickly and nobody knew exactly what was happening. Eye-witnesses later said that suddenly they **(9)** ______ Samona screaming frantically. She **(10)** ______ and was lying on the floor, her white blouse covered in blood.

Immediately Jason's brother Greg **(11)** ______ the ambulance and the police, and luckily they **(12)** ______ within a few minutes. The officers cleared the club straight away and arrested the man responsible for the stabbing. Meanwhile Samona and her boyfriend **(13)** ______ to the local hospital.

Samona needed emergency surgery, and luckily she survived. She has already recovered, but she will **(14)** ______ in hospital for at least ten days. She says she **(15)** ______ the night of the party, but who knows – perhaps it's better this way!

0. *celebrated*

1. ______

2. ______

3. ______

4. ______

5. ______

6. ______

7. ______

8. ______

9. ______

10. ______

11. ______

12. ______

13. ______

14. ______

15. ______

149 !! Banked gap fill: Bollywood

Read through the dialogue dealing with the topic of Bollywood films. Then put the verbs (A–U) into the correct gaps (1–18). But be careful because there are three extra verbs which you do not need. The first one (1) has been done for you.

Mum: Hi, darling! What was school like today?

Kim: Hi Mum! It **(1)** *was* okay, a bit tiring though. But the English lesson was great fun because we **(2)** ______ something about Bollywood.

Mum: Bollywood? That's got something to do with films, hasn't it?

Kim: Yes, that's right. Bollywood is the name of the Indian film industry. The term **(3)** ______ to Hollywood, of course. And the letter B **(4)** ______ for Bombay – the former name for Mumbai. But unlike Hollywood, Bollywood **(5)** ______ as a physical place. It only **(6)** ______ the phenomenon of Indian movies.

Mum: I see. Do American actors also **(7)** ______ in Indian films?

Kim: No, not generally. I mean there are some exceptions, of course but as a rule only Indian actors **(8)** ______ in Indian films.

Mum: Let me think ... Bollywood films **(9)** ______ a lot of music, don't they? Your dad and I, we watched such a film once, and there was constant singing and dancing.

Kim: That's true. Bollywood film music **(10)** ______ "filmi" music and it might **(11)** ______ really famous. During the last few decades Bollywood producers **(12)** ______ the soundtracks as CDs or music DVDs, hoping that the music **(13)** ______ many people watch the film in the cinema later on. So in most cases the soundtrack is way more important and more popular than the movie itself. As far as the lyrics of the songs are concerned, they aren't surprising: very often they **(14)** ______ with love and the relationship between the male and the female protagonists.

Mum: Oh, how romantic! And what about the dancing?

Kim: Well, in older Bollywood films the dancing scenes **(15)** ______ on classical Indian dance. Nowadays, however, modern elements, like those on MTV or VIVA, are mixed into the dance performances to **(16)** ______ a younger audience as well. The hero or the heroine of the film often **(17)** ______ their feelings this way, and they are usually **(18)** ______ by a troupe of dancers. Sometimes these dances are part of the plot, but this doesn't necessarily have to be so. In fact, they usually don't fit in at all!

Mum: Wow, you really do know a lot about this topic now. I'm really impressed. Maybe we should download a Bollywood movie and watch it together in the evening!

Kim: Oh no, Mum, please! Don't do that!

A	appear	B	attract	C	become
D	called	E	contain	F	deal with
G	describes	H	doesn't exist	I	ensures
J	express	K	have been releasing	L	is called
M	learned	N	performs	O	play
P	refers	Q	stands	R	supported
S	*was*	T	were based	U	will make

1	2	3	4	5	6	7	8	9
S								

10	11	12	13	14	15	16	17	18

150 !! Word formation: Bollywood

Here are some of the verbs taken from the dialogue above. Transform them into the corresponding nouns.

EXAMPLE to refer *reference*

1. to exist ....
2. to describe ....
3. to mean ....
4. to mix ....
5. to attract ....
6. to perform ....
7. to express ....

151 !! Banked gap fill: Anti-Aging

Read this interview about natural anti-aging and complete it with the verbs (the infinitives are given at the end) in the correct tense. Remember, there are two extra verbs which you do not have to use!

In times like these beauty, health and good looks *have become* more and more important. People – no matter whether they are men or women – ________________ to have the perfect body and to keep themselves fit. But unfortunately our lives ________________ busier and more stressful, so most of us ________________ the time to exercise and train regularly. The result is often disastrous: a rapid increase in weight, which almost always goes hand in hand with a feeling of being unattractive and old. If you now ____________ that plastic surgery is the only option to change the shape of our bodies and to remove wrinkles and signs of early aging, then just go on reading and ________________ how easily you might protect your body from its early decay!

First of all, ________________ or drink too much alcohol. Cigarettes ________________ nicotine, which is pure poison for your skin. Alcohol strongly ________________ to making us look old, tired and exhausted as well. Next, try to get enough sleep. An average of eight hours per night ________________ to ensure that your body and its cells ________________ enough time to regenerate. If you constantly feel tired, it's surely time to go to bed before midnight because this time of the night ________________ to have the highest relaxation effect. Moreover, make sure that you ________________ too much before you go to bed because this usually prevents you from sleeping soundly. Finally, ________________ your body on a regular basis. Three to four times a week would be perfect. Jogging and hiking are ideal sports if you want to keep fit and shape your body. But be careful not to overdo it because otherwise you ________________ the fun. If you have problems motivating yourself, ask friends or colleagues to join you. Exercising together with others ________________ you from staying at home and eating chips, crisps and cake all the time.

To summarise, it's absolutely unnecessary to undergo plastic surgery because there are easier, less expensive and less dangerous ways to stay happy, fit and healthy in a natural way! Just give it a try...! ☺

✓ to become	to find out	to recommend
to contain	to get	to say
to contribute	to have	to not smoke
to drink	to have	to spoil
to not eat	to move	to stop
to expect	to prevent	to think

152 ! Word formation: Anti-aging

Here are some nouns taken from the text above. Transform them into the corresponding adjectives.

EXAMPLE beauty *beautiful*

1. health ....
2. poison ....
3. relaxation ....
4. sleep ....
5. effect ....
6. fun ....

153 !! Word formation: Anti-aging

Here are some adjectives taken from the text above. Transform them into the corresponding nouns.

EXAMPLE important *importance*

1. perfect ....
2. disastrous ....
3. exhausted ....
4. necessary ....
5. expensive ....
6. dangerous ....
7. natural ....

154 !! Multiple choice: The Gold Rush

You are going to read a text about the gold rush in Australia. Some words are missing from the text. Choose the correct answer (A, B, C or D) for each gap (1–8). Then write your answers in the space provided. The first one (0) has been done for you.

The Australian Gold Rush – Revived

In January this year, a man walked into the Mining Exchange Gold Shop in Ballarat with a big smile on his face, **(0)** ______ a huge gold nugget in his hands. The amateur prospector **(1)** ______ the gigantic lump of gold just 63 cm below the ground near the old gold town in Victoria using a metal detector.

The nugget weighs 5,5 kg and is worth at least AUS $ 300,000 – and it shows that gold is still **(2)** ______ in the region that was the scene of the great 19th century Australian gold rush.

It all began when Edward Hargraves returned home to Sydney from California, where he **(3)** ______ for gold for years without any luck. He had a feeling that there might be gold nearer home, and in 1851 found it at Bathurst in New South Wales, on the western edge of the Great Dividing Range. That same year, gold was also found at Ballarat and Bendigo in the state of Victoria, and thousands came to the goldfields in the hope of getting rich quickly. The prospectors **(4)** ______ a licence fee to work a small plot of land, often no bigger than a boxing ring. The gold was close to the surface, so they could dig it up with picks and shovels or wash it from the rivers and creeks in pans.

The population exploded thanks to the gold rush. From 1851 to 1861, the non-Aboriginal population of Australia **(5)** ______ from 430,000 to 1,150,000. Most of the gold rush immigrants were British, but there were also other Europeans: French, Germans, Italians and Poles. Another big group were the Chinese, at 40,000. Soon Victoria produced a third of the world's gold during this period, and most of the precious metal **(6)** ______ to Britain.

For tourists today, the best thing about modern Ballarat is Sovereign Hill, an open air museum that recreates a gold town with shops, hotels, a theatre, schools, factories and mines. Characters in costume **(7)** ______ the historic buildings to life. You can take a tour of an underground gold mine, **(8)** ______ for gold youself, or learn how to load and fire a musket.

If that's all too much action, you can visit the Gold Museum instead, which has a big collection of gold coins and nuggets, nearly all of them real. One exception is the famous Welcome Nugget, which was discovered by the Red Hill Mining Company in Ballarat in 1858. At 62.85 kilos, it is the second largest gold nugget ever found. It was taken to London and displayed at Crystal Palace before it was melted down to make coins.

0	A	held	B	to hold	C	***holding***	D	having held
1	A	found	B	had found	C	found	D	founded
2	A	to be found	B	found	C	finds	D	was to be found
3	A	had searched	B	has searched	C	searched	D	had been searching
4	A	paid	B	payed	C	will pay	D	had payed
5	A	had grown	B	has grown	C	grewed	D	grew
6	A	shipped	B	was shipped	C	is shipped	D	had been shipped
7	A	are brought	B	bring	C	brings	D	will be brought
8	A	panning	B	to pan	C	pan	D	will pan

0	1	2	3	4	5	6	7	8
C								